D1498014

COMPANION
TO AN **Untold
Story**

ASSOCIATION OF WRITERS AND
WRITING PROGRAMS AWARD
FOR CREATIVE NONFICTION

COMPANION
TO AN **Untold**
Story

MARCIA ALDRICH

THE UNIVERSITY OF
GEORGIA PRESS
ATHENS AND LONDON

Published by the University of Georgia Press
Athens, Georgia 30602
www.ugapress.org
© 2012 by Marcia Aldrich
All rights reserved
Designed and typeset in 10/14 Quaadrat
by Kaelin Chappell Broaddus
Manufactured by Sheridan Books
The paper in this book meets the guidelines for
permanence and durability of the Committee on
Production Guidelines for Book Longevity of the
Council on Library Resources.

Printed in the United States of America
16 15 14 13 12 C 5 4 3 2 1

Library of Congress Cataloging-in-Publication Data
Aldrich, Marcia.
Companion to an untold story / Marcia Aldrich.
    p. cm.
ISBN 978-0-8203-4337-2 (hardocver : alk. paper) —
ISBN 0-8203-4337-4 (hardcover : alk. paper)
1. Suicide—Case studies.   2. Friendship.   I. Title.
HV6545.A53   2012
362.28'3—dc23

                                    2012006938

British Library Cataloging-in-Publication Data available

COMPANION
TO AN **Untold**
Story

Age at death. In obituaries, a proxy for the worth and fullness of the life. Joel was born May 23, 1949, and died, according to the official determination, on November 20, 1995, at age forty-six.

Aldrich, Marcia. I myself, friend, spouse, and secretary, reader, sorter, scrivener of my past, mortographer and augur, maker of lists, reciter of lines, inspector-reluctant of things the dead leave behind.

By the luck of letters I've been drawn here to the fore of the story. I have been pulled to this place with some resistance, the resistance I've felt ever since I was a child rider of the alphabet. In an essay called "The Reading," told in the third person, I portrayed my young reluctance to come to the front:

> The writers were to read in alphabetical order, just like grade school and a whole lot of other martyr-making events where because of her last name the reader had to go first. Always first in school to present her report on bread mold or Harriet Beecher Stowe, the little girl reader mumbled below hearing ("Speak up!" Miss Joy would say). Not first because of importance or merit, but first by the precision of letters' law to give the report, break the trail, take the test, hit the ball, offer herself up to the tribunal.
>
> If only the little girl reader had a name later in the alphabet. She didn't want a name like Stoppit or Testerone; they came too late and besides belonged in the pages of the grotesque, but she'd be happy to have a name ending in

the letter H. Let the ABCDEFG's exert themselves to warm up the crowd, and then turn it over to the H's for a while. But no, she was an early alphabet, a figure who for the daring required of her should be equipped with flying cape and steed. Alas no such flare and vertical capacity sprang from her spine.[1]

The second paragraph in this passage tries to catch the naive hope of a young girl who imagines a world of another order where she would escape her imposing place. And yet the little girl, for all her childish whims, intuits everything the grown woman can express, feels that her place in the alphabet comprehends all that fate has called her to, compacted to a name.

The woman knows there is no other place from which she can begin. Hit the ball, blaze the trail, saddle up to ride the alphabet, I say. ("Speak up!" Miss Joy would say.) If I have been chosen, let me choose. If I have been called to speak, let me speak with unreluctance about an unknown man, as he appears before me, looking on with inhuman eyes, as he was in the last visit, and before and after, the pivot between the friendship and the aftermath, now freed from his torn and tired life, and feel that the words are his by right, with the strength and order of letters' law.

[1] Marcia Aldrich, "The Reading." A different version of this essay appears in YOU: An Anthology of Essays in the Second Person, ed. Kim Dana Kupperman, Heather Simons, and James M. Chesbro (Gettysburg, Pa.: Welcome Table Press, 2012).

Alpha. In this book, the destination of a cross-reference—like the target of a goto statement in a programming language, or the sign to which the musician ascends in a D.S. *al fine*[2]—whence again down the page flows the river of words.

---

[2] Certain programming languages, for example C++, include a jump statement of the form "goto *label*" in which the next statement executed is the one identified by the word *label*. This means a complete transfer of control to that statement, and programmers sometimes frown upon goto as conducive to code that is hard to read and keep clean.

Dal segno al fine is also a jump statement. In sheet music it instructs the musician to navigate to the measure marked by the *segno*, a specific sign, and play to the *fine*, or end.

Ambition. His death was not the practice of resignation: "Here is the difficulty about suicide: it is an act of ambition that can be committed only when one has passed beyond ambition."[3]

[3] Cesare Pavese, *The Business of Living: Diaries, 1935–1950*, trans. A. E. Murch with Jeanne Molli (New York: Quartet, 1980), 73.

Answering machine. I have concluded that in delivering the last package the post office was too efficient (see **Last words to me**) and that Joel expected me to receive his last things when he was already dead. The box arrived like a gust of wind that through an open window ruffles papers on a desk and dies away, so that the woman who left them there, coming back to complete her task, does not notice her work has been disturbed.

The odd contents of the box, added to the evidence of Joel's prior gifts, allowed no doubt that his behavior was not in keeping with the ordinary run of things. I laid the items on the bed and showed the note to **Richard**, saying, "He isn't going to kill himself, is he?"

Richard responded as he had responded before: "Joel would never give us his things and then kill himself. He wouldn't do that to me." It would be too cruel, Richard thought, for Joel to deliver his gifts in a last visit while concealing a detailed plan of suicide. His ethics and values would not permit it.

But this time there was less conviction than anguish in Richard's voice, and he seemed to be arguing with himself, not with me. We felt, I think, the same dread anxiety.

"You should call him," I urged.

Richard phoned Joel's apartment and was relieved to hear his voice on the answering machine. Its usual message about leaving a message, delivered as it had always been, with a machine's perfect reproduction, was comforting. The words said that Joel was still alive, and not just because that is what the sound of a voice implies. It would not be Joel's way to leave this trace of himself behind.

Richard left a greeting, his voice brisk and compressed: "No need to call me back—I'll call you." When he tried again that evening, the phone rang and rang, unanswered. Joel had turned off the machine—proof that we were right, that he was still alive when the last package arrived. The package did not deliver the message it seemed to deliver, for he would not have permitted us to see unmistakable evidence of his intent before it was too late to stop him. We could have warned the police of his impending act, and they would have rushed to the apartment with sirens wailing, breaking down the door to rescue him. The very clarity of the message in the box was evidence that the message was not what it seemed.

And so by the balm of this logic anxiety was soothed, and we entered in the next days one of the periods of the story that I can least explain: the weekend and early weekdays that followed the arrival of the last things. I must have showered and dressed for work, and worked, and there were meals, and children gotten off to school and to other ordinary activities, and dogs walked, and more sleeping and bathing and dressing and working. **Thanksgiving** was coming up, with friends arriving from Ohio, a meal to plan, a house to prepare. We returned to normalcy, so much so that I can remember nothing about those days. I am invisible to myself, like a spoon dropped into a pan of dirty dishwater.

Of course we had reached the wrong conclusion about the package and the answering machine. I later asked myself, when my emotions had quieted: Where did we miscalculate? Had we misjudged Joel's wish to vanish without a trace? Did he believe his last words to me were too obscure to interpret? Only much later did I understand: The post office was too efficient, and Joel expected me to receive his last things when he was already dead.

Was Joel in the apartment at the time of Richard's call? Or did he return from a final errand and see that he had left a message? In his hollowed rooms, Joel listened to the reverberation of Richard's voice—there was no furniture to absorb the sound—saying, "No need to call me back—I'll call you." He must have shaken his head in disbelief, astounded that we still didn't get the truth, that nothing could penetrate our self-absorption and indifference. Or perhaps he thought well of such blind loyalty. He looked about his empty rooms late in the afternoon and thought, *Yes, this is my time.* He pulled the plug from the machine and got rid of it. The void was complete. His vision of a purified life had become real, and on that day he died.

Apartment. Joel's residence at 638 Athens, San Francisco, where he lived alone from 1983 until his death, the longest period of time he lived anywhere.

At the end the apartment was empty except for a gun, a phone, and a corpse. His efforts to make it a home when he had moved in twelve years earlier—rolling out carpets, hanging posters, shelving books, cutting and displaying roses—were long abandoned. Even a poor man accumulates, and the final scene was constructed by divestiture. In the months leading up to his death, he eradicated all traces of his life. He turned the pages of his best-loved books, listened one last time to the songs his mother had sung, then disposed of them for good. One last time he read his papers, letters, and notes before he stuffed them into big black bags and hauled them to the curb or burned them in a trash can out back, a bonfire of purifying destruction. He added thirty years' worth of sheet music to the common heap and set it on fire too, notes and lyrics in perfect harmony. He destroyed, sold, or gave away his lesson plans, the poetry he had written as a young man, plates and cups, coffeepot and mugs, instruction manuals and dictionaries, photographs, address book, computer, stereo, and television, clothing and toiletries, harpsichord, and car. He removed a little more of himself with each bestowal of his things, severing another connection, however fragile, to the world of the living, to his past, to us. At the end he sat cross-legged on the bare floor, the chairs and futon gone, and surveyed the emptiness around him. The room was filled by light, unabsorbed by furniture, drapes, or the objects of the living. Rid of the clutter of connection, was the final stage a fitting image of his life?

He prepared with precision and care, leaving the minimum to be faced by survivors. He wanted no one sifting through his last things. The months of planning allowed him a long, leisurely good-bye.

Arborvitae. In early October I walked home from work at the end of the day, as I always did, wondering if he had arrived and how changed we might appear to one another. In memory he was compact and taut in build, not taller than I am, with a bit of a barrel chest and a strong abdomen, moving briskly with quick, springy strides, as if the tendons in his legs were too short, and then the loose plop of his feet at the end of each step.

Our neighbor's arborvitae, twenty-five feet tall and closely planted for privacy, divided our respective properties, and each evening as I strolled homeward along the sidewalk, its plates tilted and tossed by roots of trees, my view of our front yard was blocked by the tall barrier until I was practically home. It was not until I had crossed the property line that I saw Joel, who was hoisting a Henry Weinhard beer box from his banged-up, busted dull thing of a car. For a moment he did not see me. His features were as I remembered, angular, lips thin, nose strong, eyes alive—the face of a scholar who might pore over ancient maps in a dusky archive. His black beard and coarse hair had been swept by gray and still bristled with electricity in the late strong sun. The old silver maple between the sidewalk and the street was spreading its yellow leaves on his shoulder, which was draped in a thin, shabby flannel shirt.

Then he saw me, put down his box, smiled his self-conscious smile, and walked across the grass to me. I remember that because it looked unspeakably green. It was the turning time, that summit when the red of chrysanthemums and yellow of marigolds looks deepest, endless in depth, the green leaves of the peonies from the spring darkened into a rich maroon, the hydrangea, earlier white, pink, and blue, now burnished and rattled in the wind. Snapdragons in deep crimson and pale apple-blossom pink still bloomed among the blue reblooming delphiniums and the unabated burgundy of stonecrop.

In a few days everything would change. The yellow marigolds would wizen, the hectic leaves of maple would crisp and brown and catch on windowsills, the trees nearly bare and colorless, the flowerbeds hollow. But not yet. His hug was warm and heartfelt, and mine was too. He had aged, was frail in a way I was not, not in frame and muscle, not in a debility of will.

Augury. Divination by omens, in particular the behavior of birds, an art known to Roman priests and others in the ancient world. Especially meaningful were birds in flight,[4] a swerve to the left or right, and their cackles and caws, and the pecking patterns of certain sacred chickens, and entrails were read. The priests, the augurs, did not predict the future in a general way, but interpreted signs that told the fate of a specific course of action, which, Romans being Romans, was usually a military or political one. It would not serve to go against the gods, and a blessing or warning could be gleaned by those who watched with care for an ominous eagle.

[4] "For a bird of the air shall carry the voice, and that which hath wings shall tell the matter" (Eccles. 10:20).

August 21, 1995. Date of our return from six weeks in London and the British Isles. A few days later Joel called to say that he was going to visit us. It would be the first time in more than ten years, should the trip pan out. During that decade we had offered many invitations, heard the expression of many wishes to accept. Plans were brewed. But in the end Joel had always pleaded poverty too great to permit travel: "You've been expecting word that I've determined that a trip east is unaffordable, and I don't want needlessly to prolong your anticipation: I can't afford the trip. Of course, I can't really afford to stay here, either. All in all, living has seemed an unjustifiable extravagance."[5] He worked as a substitute teacher and home tutor in a school district south of San Francisco, riding on the lip of indigence just ahead of flat broke.

The call in August differed from other bruited visits in that Joel stated firmly he would arrive, but didn't know exactly when. It seemed an odd way to proceed. Generally speaking, a definite plan to travel includes a specific schedule. So despite the firmness of his assertions, we treated the announced visit with skepticism, expecting it to come to naught. We did not really believe in it until Joel called from Illinois on October 4 to say that he would reach our house the next day.

[5] Letter, July 12, 1989. Unless otherwise indicated, all letters are from Joel to Richard.

During the August phone call he said that he was undertaking a major housecleaning, divesting himself of items he had kept since childhood for who knows what purpose, and that he'd bring some of these items along. He would send a list of books and wanted Richard to check off those he'd like Joel to transport. He was giving us his computer and would rediscover the pleasures of handwriting. He spoke energetically about the purification ritual, the good effect of ridding himself of accumulated sundries. Our children were as close to family as he had, and he wanted them to have his possessions—that was how he put it.

Auto. A word in constellation with *self* and *suicide*, a fatal auto crack-up.

```
      BELL MARKETS #1
        1390 SILVER AVE.
    08/04 12:12PM STORE     271
    CU  101 REG  3 OPR      117

  MED SALSA              2.09*
    1.79LB @ .99/ LB
  RED FLAME GRAPES       1.77*
        MEAT             2.32*
  WALNUT COOKY           2.19*
    1.18LB @ .59/ LB
  RED ONIONS              .70*
     .60LB @ .39/ LB
  CARROTS LOOSE           .23*
  HEAD LETTUCE            .69*
    3.72LB @ .49/ LB
  PINEAPPLES             1.82*
     .43LB @ 3.59/ LB
  RED BELL PEPPERS       1.54*
    1.04LB @ .79/ LB
  SMALL TOMATOES          .82*
        GROCERY          2.69*
         TOTAL          16.86
        CASH TEND       20.06

      3.20 CHANGE

    THANKS FOR COMING IN
```

Awake. "At 8:00 this morning, I was in line at Bell Market, morally aglow. I was early to rise to my homely duties. My oranges were chosen for thin skins and minimal navels; my chicken would tax neither my vascular system nor my wallet; the yogurt was plain and would be only lightly embellished with the Spreadable Fruit in the 10-oz. jar I will make last a month; my bread was loaded with bran. As I walked my bag to the car, I could hardly avoid thinking what a wonderful lesson I could teach the world if only it were awake to see me."[6]

[6] Letter, June 9, 1990.

Banal suicide. Writ small, committed in private space, offstage, not performed, resistant to mythology, unnoticed, unrecorded, a minor thing.

Impossible to romanticize or mythologize a suicide carried out in the most private room of the house: the bathroom, a space off-limits even to other family members, where dissocial acts are performed in solitude.

The dull setting of his final act was appropriate to his station in life. Joel was not a celebrated figure, someone of public note. He was a substitute teacher—someone never to become permanent.

But even a famous figure can exit stage banal. The barnstorming poet Vachel Lindsay, who chanted his verse before thousands, drank a bottle of Lysol in the bathroom.

Barbara. Joel's friend in his last years, an acquaintance made in teaching. She took one of the last photos of Joel, in which, lowering his eyes from the camera, he holds her dog Pepper. She sent the photo to Richard when he contacted her to find out if she knew about Joel's death. I then wrote to her, asking follow-up questions of a research sort, to which she responded:

> Joel had a lot of friends who didn't know each other. Just after his death, I met with a teacher pal of his whom he had talked about for years. We had an awkward brunch, realizing (at least on my end) that we had nothing, really, in common, except for this mutual friend. We both had anticipated (I think) that we would be more "in synch." (If A likes B, and B likes C, then A must like C . . .)
>
> This separation of spheres of friendship enabled Joel to carry out his last "rites" without any single party knowing the whole story. If it's any consolation, I truly believe Joel felt a sense of gratification about having hatched a perfect plan (over decades, probably)—everything was handled to the last detail. Since he often felt inadequate in life, he may have been (perversely) elated to manage this massive task so competently and effectively.

As far as your book goes, the project (as you describe it) appears to be your method of working through your feelings about the suicide. Which is great. I'm all for it. But that process is personal to you, and not really my business. Honestly, I don't feel much drawn to sitting down and answering those questions, especially if they're intended to fill the gaps for a book. On other hand, I would be open to helping in a different way. If you would like to have a personal conversation on the phone, approaching the subject from your heart in order to clarify your own feelings and thoughts, that would make sense to me. The point is, if you would like to make contact for yourself (your book aside), I'm more than happy to share my experiences with you. But I don't want to be part of a bibliography.

Suicide is traumatic for everyone it touches, and emotions can be severe. I hope that you are feeling close to resolving any feelings that have remained over past years. I think Joel loved the two of you and I'm sure that, if there were any place from which his spirit could look back on the living, he would regret having caused pain.

Good luck. Take care. And call if you want to (leave a message—I'm often screening!).

Barbara[7]

[7] Barbara, e-mail to me, December 2, 2004.

Bartleby. In his soul a bit of a clerk. —PHILIP ROTH

Bathroom (1). The bathroom had technical advantages as the final choice of occupancy. Having lived alone in obscurity, Joel knew that no one would come upon him in the normal course of events, no child or spouse or parent or lover or friend who would be devastated by the discovery. No stranger could see into this room without windows, set back from the street and reached through a locked garage. The sound of the gunshot would be muffled. Yet it would be the first room police would encounter opposite the front door. He did not want to draw out the search that would be conducted to find him. He would be considerate in his last act, minimizing the trouble his death would cause, minimizing the emotional trauma too. He knew there could be copious amounts of blood, easily cleaned on the bathroom's forgiving floor. He chose a place where signs of his presence could be erased. Stains on tiles are temporary.

Viewless, bookless, laid with cold linoleum, at once the most ritualistic and impersonal room in the apartment, stripped down to its dull tiles, not even a towel or toothbrush to remind him of the years he had lived there—it was the fitting spot to commit what many would call an inhuman act. Where he made his daily routine of cleansing was the best place for his last cleansing. Not the living room with its partial carpet, nor the open and unconcealing kitchen, not the second room with its view to the garden roses and growth and renewal. The second room would have been an ironic choice, and while Joel was a deeply ironic man, he was not ironic about roses. In those final moments, the roses might have distracted him.

Bathroom (2). Where I retreat for privacy in times of emotional despair. I cry in the shower, the tears I shed flowing down the drain and underneath the city streets to the river, which runs to the lake and perhaps some sea. I can curl like a fetus on the cold floor, leaving no residue of turmoil. In bathrooms everything is washed away.

Bed. Device of rest and procreation. Before I met Richard, I slept in many beds but belonged to none. Most often I slept in single beds, many of them uncomfortable, unfit for dreams, as if stuffed with stones. Here and there I shared a bed, but the experience did not alter my essential solitude or transient life. The only notable bed of my adulthood has been the **bed of metamorphosis.**

Bed of metamorphosis. Our bed was once Joel's, purchased with **Gale** at a big indoor flea market on Ventura Boulevard in Sherman Oaks, just a few blocks from where Richard lived. It was a water bed, and on one of the pieces of plywood that formed the foundation for the mattress was written in red marker *Natural enviorments only*—a sign of passion in manufacture and of confusion in spelling. The plywood was supported by four lengths of pressboard, each notched in the middle so that two pieces, laid on edge, slid into one another to form an X. Four longer pieces of pressboard, painted black, made the outer base, and then on top was set a heavy frame of thick, rough-hewn pine, darkly stained, with a Spanish tile inlaid on the headboard and another on the footboard. It all came apart and went back together again.

Joel and Gale hauled the bed up to Santa Barbara, where they were students at the university and later joint dropouts from it. It was their bed, and they lay down in it together in the small house at **1635 San Andres Street**. "We've finally got our waterbed inflated and slept-upon," Joel wrote with a tone of domestic pleasure.[8]

But their residence in the house together was brief. When Joel and Gale faltered, she left the bed behind, and she was

[8] Letter, August 28, 1973.

uninvolved in its disposition. Stained with dark loss, it became anathema to Joel. He did not want to be reminded of aborted love, and he pushed the bed out the door and onto another sea. It passed to Richard and traveled back to Sherman Oaks. Joel, for the rest of his days, slept on a fold-up couch.

Richard took the bed with him from home to home, California and Northwest, Appalachia and Midwest. It was still our bed during Joel's **last visit**, when he helped move it back into the bedroom after new carpet was installed.

Beginning. A note on appearance was my first writing about Joel. He isn't mentioned, though his presence, or I should say his absence, infuses the whole. I didn't begin with the facts but with my own blindness, as if that was the first cause, the thing I most had to grapple with:

> What I see is people going about their lives like clockwork. They get up in the morning, every morning without fail, and begin their days—retired couples who swim every morning at seven, men and women walking their dog before work, a woman hauling out the trash. Kids are gotten off to school, errands are run, cars pull out of driveways. Later in the day children are picked up, trash bins are hauled back in from the curb, dinner is started, laundry is folded, homework is supervised, phone calls answered, bills paid, and bed is retired to. This is what I see—lives functioning, functioning lives. Clockwork. No skipped beats. No one suspended in time. No one poised in the in-between.
>
> No one speaks of unhappiness or divorce or disappointment. Despair, loneliness, and pain happen offstage, in the wings, behind heavy curtains. No one stands outside her house, unable to enter. If someone drives aimlessly

about after work, not wanting to go home, I don't know it. If financial disaster looms, if jobs are dreaded and children are crying themselves to sleep, I don't know it. If suicide is being contemplated, planned, or executed, I don't know it.

The Substitute Teacher

1   What I see is people going about their lives like clockwork. They get up in the morning, every morning without fail, and begin their days--retired couples who swim every morning at seven, men and women walking their dog before work, a woman hauling out the trash. They make breakfast, get dressed, writers write, kids are gotten off to school, errands are run, cars pull out of driveways. Later children are picked up, or parents wait at home for children to walk in the door, trash bins are hauled back in from the curb, again dogs are walked, children are driven to piano lessons or soccer practices, homework supervised, trips made to the market, dinner started, meals eaten and cleaned, laundry put away, floors swept, newspapers read, phone calls answered, bills paid, t.v. watched, and then they retire to bed. This is what I see--lives functioning, functioning lives. Clockwork.
       I don't see domestic squabbles, I don't see couples arguing over morning coffee, I don't see heads held in despair, I don't see people staring ahead blankly, I don't see people unable to get out of bed or return home at the end of the day, people aren't locking themselves in bathrooms or pouring another drink, I don't

---

The second entry in what I called "The Substitute Teacher" leaps ahead to the autumn after Joel's death, when I accidentally struck a boy who ran in front of my car (see Path [2]). An illusion about myself was shattered: the illusion that I couldn't hurt anyone, that I had control over my life. Another veil had been lifted from my eyes. Terrible things can happen in which I am implicated.

---

last there remains a single thread of self, immaculate and singing.
       He knew me, could talk with difficulty. I put the flowers near his bed where he could see them .
       That eveing, around seven, as I drove my daughter to the high school to drop her off at a football game, I ran into a young boy with my car. I turned the corner onto the street fronting the high school where cars were pulling to the side of the road to let their kids out. From nowhere a young boy ran out right in front of my car. I was driving slowly, even so I couldn't brake or swerve out of his path. I hit him although it seemed more that he ran into me. I heard a thud and then he bounced to the side of the road. He lay on the curb for just a second in which I thought my heart would explode, and then he sprang up again. I pulled off jaggedly, sticking half into the road, and ran to him. His father was running to his son at the same time. By the time I reached him, his father had his

---

Joel, again, is barely mentioned in the entry.

Berkeley. The University of California, Berkeley. In Joel's mind, *the University*, a proper name. Though he politely used the same term in connection with the institutions that granted degrees to Richard and me, in that usage the word was lowercase, generic, flat, discharged, drained. Had occasion presented itself, he might have conceded worth to the elite eastern schools, but they were not his name brand, and Joel never mentioned them. None of them was Berkeley in the sixties, when hot rhetoric and tear gas blew from Sproul Plaza into laboratories that had precipitated the Nobel Prize.

It was one of the conditions of Berkeley's preeminence that his brother, Michael, went there: AB (1966), MA (1967), PhD (1971)—all in economics. (Joel, were he listing these degrees, would have substituted "baccalaureate," "master's," and "doctorate." He was the only person I have ever known to say "baccalaureate" in casual talk.)

Joel's attitude about Berkeley was not a pure snobbery, but his own peculiar mix of particles in tension: a constricted sense of the best of a kind, a feeling of incapacity to achieve the best of a kind, and a distaste for that which was less than the best of its kind. This stable but noxious habit of feeling was a defining fact of his self-catastrophe.

In 1978 Joel earned a BA in English from Berkeley. See **Higher education.**

Better world. "My last day sub-ing was sometime in early May, I think. No matter: regardless how seldom you do it, you never forget how; it's just like retching. I try, from time to time, to figure out a plan for public education that I could live with, but never come up with a system that serves even in the most general terms. I'm inhibited by something like an abysmal sense of futility: I feel helplessly at odds with the world as it is, but its imperfections seem to be what allows me even the limited crevice I've occupied most of my adult life; when I try to imagine a better world, there really isn't a place for me, at all."[9]

[9] Letter, August 28, 1990.

Beyond Insight. A book by
Sumner L. Shapiro,
Joel's childhood analyst,
a follow-up to *Moment
of Insight: Vignettes from
a Psychoanalytic Practice*, written at a time when psychoanalysis,
like a Rust Belt manufacturer whose labor costs are too high,
was losing market share to newer therapies: Rogerian,[10] neo-
Jungian, post-Adlerian, mystic, yogic, behaviorist, rebirthing,
Rolfing, primal screaming, transactional analysis, EST, and,
of course, psychotropic drugging, even so early in our Age of
Pharmaceuticals.

As part of his grievous efforts to make sense of Joel's history, Richard bought a copy of *Beyond Insight* from a used-book
seller, in farfetched hope that he might find Joel within its
fictionalized covers. However, Dr. Shapiro had sent Joel a copy
when the volume was published in 1979—a gift to which he
reacted with disgust—and, proud author or no, hardly would
have subjected Joel to a disguised,
heightened, dramatized, and
vignettized portrait of himself.

[10] "School. Yes, I hassled my way
through another day of showing
unconditional positive regard for
everyone" (letter, June 25, 1984).

Joel had his own moment of insight, "an early-life experience with reality—I suffered a premature intuition of adult human nature—was punished in my adolescence by exposure to psychiatric mind-diminution."[11] (For more on this insight, see **Chain, chain, chain.**) Joel was not always so dismissive of therapy as a punishment by shrinkage. In the high school days of their friendship, perhaps while he was still seeing Dr. Shapiro, he had in conversation offered Richard—ready with his native or nurtured skepticism—a Freudian interpretation of the wet, soft particles of torn napkin he rolled in his fingers as they sat at the kitchen table. In fact, Joel was in group therapy, "still fighting the battle against myself to which I devoted myself when I undertook to become a teacher,"[12] at the time of his dismissive remark about his time with Dr. Shapiro. And years before that remark, Joel had seen another shrink, learning something about his lifetime difficulty in recalling the names of people, whether acquaintances or authors: "It's scarier than shit on a poorly lit Berkeley sidewalk, suddenly to realize that I've been so caught-up in myself that I've been unable to remember other people's names."[13] In his last year this hole in memory grew.

[11] Letter, February 26, 1982.
For more on his absorption
by therapy, see **Spin the bottle.**
[12] Letter, April 18, 1982.
[13] Letter, November 1975.

Binoculars. Uncomfortable and intrusive things. I didn't buy them in a fit of bird-watching zeal, nor were they given to me brand new. They aren't very good binoculars. In their day they might have been fine for a child. They're compact, fit for a narrow face and eye span. Too small for my husband's broad face, they adjust perfectly to me.

As I ease them from their cracked case of imitation leather, the cool hardness in my hands is like a thing lifted from the shelf in a dank basement, chilled jars of pickles or plums or pears—no, more like an ancient, hard-shell Samsonite suitcase brought up from the bowels of the house and into the light.[14] A long black strap attaches to the squat case for portage in the fields. The Velcro patch that holds the top flap down is remarkably fresh and makes a loud scratchy sound when I pull it open. The binoculars were manufactured by Jason, Empire Model 219, the name emblazoned on the two eyepiece caps remaining of the original four. I keep the binoculars in their protective case on a shelf with my cookbooks in the family room. No matter what time of day I reach for them, what time of year, they're cold to the touch and unforgiving, my binoculars.

[14] See Marcia Aldrich, "The Mother Bed," *Gettysburg Review* 20, no. 4 (2007): 509–18.

Birthday. "Deer coming through," Richard calls out from the kitchen. Eight deer in a line walk slowly through the snow-filled yard in back just before seven in the morning. The dark is vanishing, and the scene is lit by the night's fallen snow, heavy on the trees and shrubs. I've just gotten out of the shower, my head wrapped with a towel. I rip the towel off so I can put my glasses on to see, grab my bathrobe off the hook, and run downstairs to get my binoculars from their shelf. The last deer in the procession, the smallest, a fawn, isn't moving like the others, although none is moving fast this early morning at the end of a long and cold February. It's been one of the snowiest months on record, so cold we haven't seen the deer much. They tend to huddle somewhere in the woods, I imagine, burrowed into hollows together to collect their heat against the winds. When it begins to warm up at the beginning of spring, the deer appear across the river. But here they are in the cold, looking for forage they missed in several prior passes through our yard.

The hind legs of the fawn are reedy, stiff, and dragging, while its companions are more elastic. And he's falling behind.

It's my birthday, and after wishing me a happy day, Richard says, "I bet five years ago you didn't think you'd be watching deer passing through your backyard on your birthday." He knows I love deer and says it to mark the occasion as happy. And it is happy. Yet these deer are not perfect figurines, complacent in my yard like statues. They are not postcard deer, not decoration to my new rural life, exhibits for observation. They are real deer who are emaciated from months of little food, and they are cold deer from living in conditions we humans devote ourselves to avoiding. And the hindmost fawn is moving haltingly.

I want to feed the deer in the winter, I want to spread grain on the snow, sprinkle corn and apples. Our neighbors feed the ducks, which struggle up the icy banks of the river and scrape across the snow to the feeder. On the less cold winter days an old warrior raccoon, whose back legs have incurred some challenge, a fall from a tree or blow from an automobile, warily eases his way down the tree where he nests by the river. He drags across our yard to our neighbors' feeder, scattering the ducks.

Richard thinks it's wrong to interfere with the ecosystem around the **river house**, that we humans do more harm than good wading into matters we don't understand, and I restrain myself. I don't feed the wildlife, not the ducks, not the deer, not the emaciated fawn with legs like dry wild grass.

Breathless. On the phone Joel sounded breathless, as if the rarity of human exchange made him anxious—or perhaps he was excited at the contact. In his last years, he became more and more oblique and fragmentary in conversation and could or would not tell a story that I could follow. He deflected talk from topics he didn't want to discuss. This was especially true with regard to employment. He had from long years of essential solitude fallen out of the habits of social relations less confined than the strictly professional, or had chosen to ignore their parameters because he had become exclusive to himself, disassembling the rudiments of interaction.

Or perhaps he found all conversation stressful because, as he claimed, the medications he took to block the pain of neuropathy (see **Neuropathy, diabetic**) confused his grammar and memory.

In any case, the result was that we knew little about the actualities of Joel's life. When we attempted to find out, to pose questions, to follow up a glancing suggestion, we ran into a wall. He was Melville's Bartleby; he preferred not to speak of it. His obscure talk reflected his sense of his life—a sidelong look of the briefest duration was all it merited.

Buji. Literary publication of Reseda High School, under the direction of Bernard Goodman ("Bernie" to Joel), with an Eastern tone, under the discipline of the haiku and other short forms meant to ward off the grand effusions of poets composing at the hormonal age.[15]

[15] "As an example of how miserably my mind has been working, I was thinking in the wee hours last night of Buji, trying to recollect what the word means ('good luck'?)" (letter, August 19, 1990). D. T. Suzuki, a major interpreter of Zen for the Beats, comments, "When the Dharma is truly, fully, and existentially (experientially) understood, we find that there is nothing wanting in this life as we live it. Everything and anything we need is here with us and in us. One who has actually experienced this is called a man of *buji*. . . . Ji (*shih*) generally means 'business,' 'event,' 'matter,' 'concern,' 'engagement,' 'affair,' etc. When all this is negated [by the addition of *bu-*], we may have for 'a man of *buji*' 'one who has no business,' or 'one to whom no events happen,' or 'one who is unconcerned or indifferent or disinterested,' or 'one to whom nothing matters,' and so on. But 'a man of *buji*' is not any of them. He is the one who has a true understanding of the Dharma or Reality" (Daisetz T. Suzuki, "Rinzai on Zen," *Chicago Review* 12, no. 2 [1958]: 14–15 n. 7).

In *Buji Twice*, the second issue, from summer 1966, Joel placed four poems largely concerned with immensity, as in this haiku:

In the vast ocean
An aged fish swims, searching
For tears he once shed.

In the third *Buji*, from 1967, Joel was assistant editor and contributed fourteen poems, among them this intensely rhyming octave:

I love you
No matter what I am to you;
Whether I am to you what I do
Or what I want to;
No matter what you feel,
No matter what you feel.
I am what I feel
For you.

There were no poems by Joel in the fourth issue of *Buji*, for by then he had dropped out of school.

Bullet. The penetrating cause of death. It was deformed in its passage through bone and tissue, measuring 1.3 × 0.7 cm at the base when recovered in the autopsy.

In some attempted suicides, the would-be victim manages to fire the gun but quails at the final moment, wrecking face or skull but surviving. Not Joel, a performer whose hands trembled at the harpsichord. He made an excellent approximation to a perfect level shot.

Buteo regalis. Death in the making, in the form of an old black cat with green eyes, curled in the curve of my arm, in the hollow space between Richard and me in the marital bed, the cradle of light, labored breathing, still it was, facing me with a face, all through the night when suddenly up it got and vomited on the spread, and then moved to the corner, no food or water would it take; it had nothing left to say, still it moved from place to place searching . . . for a final resting place? a last anchor? a place to be alone, I think . . . offstage. But I wouldn't let it be alone, no, I had to search for it, look in all the old places, up in the attic in the eaves, under the back porch ruins, opening and closing doors, until I found it huddling outside. I had to put my arms around it, small it was . . . near the end . . . there had been so much more in my memory, and I had to embrace it, hold it, not let it go. Father called then and I couldn't answer, I could hear the rings through the windows, I knew it was him, I always know when it is Father calling, he knows when not to call, and calls, has an uncanny sense when I am in the throes of something. . . . This is when he calls, I can count on it. I can count on what he'll say if I answer too. . . . *Oh you and your deaths*, he'll say as if I collect them. . . . Maybe I do; what's to be done about it, I can't help things don't last, I can't help I'm in the thick of things going to ruin, and he lets the phone

ring such a long time, eternity really, refusing to accept that I
won't answer, that he can't wear me down, why don't I answer,
well, I could say I was outside, holding the huddling thing,
putting my arms around it, but I could have let go and gone
inside and answered, all right, I didn't answer because I didn't
want to and I didn't want to because I don't like lying, I can't
say . . . everything is wonderful . . . lilacs blowing . . . ducks
swimming . . . happy day . . . that kind of thing, I can't and
that's what Father wants and when he doesn't get happy day,
he lets me have it, *Oh you and your deaths* . . . that's what he
says with boredom and condescension dripping from his
voice . . . so no . . . I didn't answer, I was busy hugging the huddling thing, and then the strangest thing happened . . . a bunch
of tiny birds, sparrows, flew about the tree, out of nowhere,
ten I should think, they were making an awful noise, half past
noon it was . . . what was it, I wondered, that stirred them, then
I saw . . . the *Buteo regalis* . . . all ruffled, all turned out . . . *kree-a*
kree-a . . . compact, legs rusted and ruffled, lots of white, juve-
nile it was, still green about the killing, saw its white legs
landing in the grass by the tree lit with sparrows, the sparrows
were dive-bombing the hawk . . . he held his ground, a small
emperor, the wind picked up . . . a bottle far away rattled as it
rolled down a hill, the way things that need to flow downward
do, and the sparrows were up and swooping, the sun came
out from behind the clouds, everything ablaze with light, the
hawk still in the grass, *dominion* that's the word I thought, was
I sparrow or hawk . . . was I one . . . or the other, which face did
I wear as the hawk flew up, sparrows in tow, his royal retinue,
from tree to tree, they flew . . . and then out of sight, the sun
disappeared, the sky thickened, wind grew and grew, building;
branches began to break and pitch down, a few drops of rain,
no more, I expected downpour, I expected the river to overflow
its banks, but . . . no . . . a few drops . . . a sprinkling, on and

off . . . all through the day until night like an intermittent suitor
who comes and goes and can't decide whether to stay, still I
didn't answer my father's call *Oh you and your deaths*, I picked
up the branches, dragging the big ones to the bank of the
river, adding them to the pile, I went inside and changed the
sheets . . . pulled them off the bed, tried to dry the damp place
on the spread, I remade the bed and got in, the spread still
damp, I could feel it.

Cassanego. The officer who was dispatched on a well-being check to Joel's apartment when the police received his **suicide note**. With no response to his knocks at the front door, Cassanego unlocked it, using the key Joel had sent along with the note. Cassanego found Joel in the bathroom, lying in his own blood, and called an ambulance. See **Police report**.

Cause of death. A juridical concept. All official deaths must have a cause. If a person dies at home and the police cannot arrange for a medical professional (such as the deceased's doctor) to specify a cause, an autopsy is performed. Thus Joel became Coroner's Case No. 1475-95. The autopsy established cause and mode of death.

The medical cause of death was determined to be:

PENETRATING CLOSE CONTACT
GUNSHOT WOUND OF HEAD.

The mode of death was determined to be:

SUICIDE.

Certificate of death. Formal proof of passing on. The pronounce-ment of death by an authorized person determines the official date and time, which may differ from the moment of physi-ological death. Joel may have died three days before the official date. See **Rigor mortis.**

Joel's father forwarded a copy of the certificate of death to Richard, along with forms from the California State Teachers' Retirement System, or CalSTRS, since Richard was the desig-nated beneficiary. The lump-sum distribution, as it was called, amounted to $1,544.37 after taxes, money we used to purchase the **Steinway Model K.**

This preliminary version of the certificate, issued prior to the autopsy, lists under item 107, "Death was caused by," the fol-lowing (with quotation marks):

"Pending"
"Further Investigation and/or Testing"

Other areas of the certificate have the force of blunt pre-cision. Under item 12, "Occupation," Joel is identified as a "Teacher," with 20 years (item 19) in the practice of "Education," his "Kind of Business" (item 18).

These solitary terms in allotted spaces, the checkbox options of Yes or No, these digits—they do not feed my hunger for facts, the solace of the real, for explanation and verification, truth told about this unknown man whom we knew, a steadfast mourning. The certificate of death, with its certainty and emptiness, would make a fine figure in this companion. But the Office of Vital Records, for reasons of privacy, refused permission to reproduce it.

Chain, chain, chain. How did Joel assess, how did he feel about his mother's death? His overt response was to blame his father (see **Prell, Ruth Sosin**). A few months after her suicide, having moved north to start school at Berkeley, Joel described her as a star in a loveless constellation.

> And so I get around to telling you what maybe you already know—that I'm really hurting in places I can't even begin to reach, places way in the past and in a fugitive present. My memory is not trustworthy, in general, but I do remember clearly that, by the age of eleven, I was spending lots of time crying and murmuring into my pillow about no one loving me. Later, my crying and murmuring was aimed at specific individuals [it becomes clear two sentences later that he means his parents] and by my second year of high school had begun to be expressive of a skepticism about the existence of love. Maybe I've got the order a bit confused, but at some point near the time of that skeptical turn, I began to wonder, to doubt, if I, myself, was capable of love. And not too long after that, I began to understand things about my parents I'd known since the first time I filled my pillow in a fit of seemingly irrational tears.

Joel at the time of these reflections was taking English 1A in his first quarter at Berkeley and wrote his first essay about his mother.

> The lack of love in her life destroyed her. Until the last months, I had not fully understood that her parents had brought her up in an absence or frustration of love, and that, in fact, her mother had, during the last years, perverted the idea of love into a self-serving claim on my mother's obligations to her. Everyone wondered why my mother was so upset by my grandmother's problems with the nursing homes and such. There's no mystery. She wanted to believe she had those obligations, that mother-daughter love had existed between them. Of course, she couldn't reconcile that need with her bitterness toward the woman who she believed had denied her both motherly love and, by dominating her father, fatherly love. The whole matter of family love-roots was unmediated by any balancing love in her own family's life, built as it was around a vacuous marriage. . . . It is hard for me not to wonder if, growing up in this chain of failure-of-love, I'm not doomed to failure as well.[16]

In this light, the asseveration of love in the brave Buji octave—love for the addressee whether she loves back or not—appears to be a futile effort at self-levitation.

[16] Letter, December 13, 1975.

Circle. Image used to make concrete the distinction between inclusion and exclusion. A fine example is Edwin Markham's "He drew a circle that shut me out." In planning his own death, Joel changed from the man we had long known, redrawing the geometry of his communication, while Richard continued to operate within the bounded circle of intimacy they had shared for decades. Joel's perspective now lay outside that circle. Like a credulous Horatio, Richard continued to believe that Joel would not behave so cruelly as he in fact behaved—until the tragic end proved him the fool (see **Role**).

"You're the only one I tell the truth to," he told Richard. He lied.

Clare and David. My daughter and son, ages eleven and seven at the time of Joel's last visit. On the day he arrived, David's first new bed was delivered by the furniture store, replacing the corroded brass headboard donated by my older sister. It was hard for David to see the new cherry bed carried into the house and up the stairs to his room, knowing that Joel would sleep in it first. I told the deliverymen to set up the dark lustrous frame against the wall near the front window, where Joel could look out onto the silver maple, see the yellow globes of the streetlights go on, peer down to the flowerbeds still aglow or beaded with morning dew, and observe the paths of people on the sidewalks, wending their way to somewhere.

And so was the last visit framed by beds new and old (see **Reassembly**).

The children saw the shabbiness he wore, the holes in his socks, the ragged straps on his sandals, shirts frayed to a state of transparency, his khaki jacket of a windbreaker weight, and felt a child's tenderness for him, like a fledgling fallen from its nest. "He needs a warmer jacket. Give him a warmer jacket," Clare urged. The children snuck into his room to lay extra blankets on the new bed. "He seems so cold," the children said. "He is so in need of covering."

Clementine. A favorite fruit served to Joel during his last visit. He said, "I've never tasted anything so sweet and bitter at the same time. And the smell lingers long after they are gone." I see curled peels heaped in mounds.

Collector's "I." From the mundane to the exotic, from the useful to the useless, the collectible is tangible, and that is its point. You can see, touch, categorize, and name it. However, it is not the thing itself, but the eye cast upon the thing, that makes it collectible. Baseball cards, knives, rare books, African masks, ceramic eggs, hats, dolls, or nutcrackers in collections are not treated like common things, used to slice a melon or keep off the sun, but hung on walls, displayed in glass cases, protected in binders. They are often cataloged by collectors who proceed with full purpose, who have a view of what they are building, seeking specific items to fill in gaps and achieve complete coverage. But no collection is ever completed, because want of the desired object is the essence of collecting, and you cannot want what you already have. With some collectibles, say salt shakers, there can be no thought of completion, for they are stars in the limitless sky. But the same law of desire applies when the collected objects are restricted in number. A collector who gathered all the David Winter cottages, when they were a niche mania, waited eagerly for new designs yet to be issued. When new cottages ceased, so did the mania. In possession of each buffalo nickel, a numismatist would seek finer specimens of the coins he already possessed or widen his horizon to pennies and dimes.

With all collections, the desired items cast back the light of the eye that looks on them. The collector says, "I collect rare books" or "I collect African masks." The collector says, "I am a collector."

Colma. A city of crypts. It buries the dead of San Francisco, which prohibits graveyards within its limits (the only exceptions are the national cemetery in the Presidio and the tiny walled garden within Mission Dolores, featured in Hitchcock's *Vertigo*). Joel drove past, and sometimes through, the necropolis-city on his commute to teach in South San Francisco: "This morning, I flipped an illegal U-turn in avoidance of a half-hour fight for the on-ramp and drove through Colma, death's acres, on my alternate way to work. One of the cemeteries struck me as remarkable. The markers are set flat in the ground, and flowers, presumably placed on graves, look like wind-strewn clumps of garbage. There was one person visiting the place and it was striking how incongruous any but a ragged, dusty being looks there. There's no imagined scent of a widow's perfume."[17] This alternate way to work was probably via El Camino Real, which would have taken him through Colma's Woodlawn Memorial Park, where he was ultimately interred in the Rose Garden, and where his secrets came to rest. No generations of family gathered for the occasion, no friends to tell stories of outlandish pranks, there was no grand hurrah, no memorial service, no viewing, no scattering of ashes, no widow scented by perfume.

[17] Letter, June 9, 1990.

Contact person. Michael, Joel's brother, made the final arrange-
ments. He told the police that Joel had been depressed about
his landlord's plans to sell his building. Joel didn't say a word
on that subject to us.

Cryptic. Descriptive of a technique of diversion. Even Joel's expressions of personal reflection were cryptic: "This weekend, I confessed something of the truth about my self to myself. I cannot speak of it. Have you ever felt sympathy with a sock that wants to be turned right side out?"[18] To ask for more about this truth was to ask a man who had already retired from the scene, to ask about a vault, a great vacancy he continued to inhabit.

[18] Letter, February 27, 1984.

Data. I can imagine someone else, an investigative reporter, getting to know the sources, interviewing people, gathering data in an organized fashion.[19] This person would have distance and therefore treat the material more objectively, less personally, perhaps as a sociological profile on suicide. She would be armed to fill in the factual holes, track down medical records, present the data.

I can imagine that person in the abstract, but in reality there is no one but me who cares to write. Mine is not the assemblage of an exhaustive account. From the outset I have believed I was trying to write a story about the story, to be in its company. I can't piece together a seamless, coherent account. Just the opposite. This is a record of my struggle with Joel's struggle and indicates the limits of what I know and what I understand.

[19] In 1999, submitting a grant proposal, I knew I was not this person: "This is no conventional case history, no objective investigation into a suicide in America at the end of the twentieth century. I am no expert on the subject, in the technical sense, having no degree in sociology or psychology. I am not a coroner or clinician. I will not serve up tables with definitive statistics, no demographic breakdowns or age charts. My book gives an antiromantic, antimythologizing treatment to the sober subject of suicide. It is part elegy, part biography, part meditation, part philosophical speculation, part self-interrogation. It is nonlinear, discontinuous, a mosaic of entries, subjects braided together of irregular lengths and styles. Most are brief."

Death of a Salesman. A play much taught in schools. Arthur
Miller innovates in making the protagonist of his tragedy
not the typical prince but a low man, Willy Loman, to whom,
though he leaves behind no monument to his industry and talent, attention must be paid.

In April 1984, Joel, now thirty-four years old, had a three-day
stint substitute-teaching the play to an English class at South
San Francisco High. It was, he said, "chock full of themes and
characters perfectly designed to make me miserable at this
moment in my life."[20] The sore spots are apparent in Miller's
plot of two brothers in rivalry for their father's love and blessing. Says Biff to Happy, "Not finding yourself at the age of
thirty-four is a disgrace!"[21]

Joel's own brother was Michael, some four years older and
his lone sibling. "There was . . . intense competition with
Michael," Gale commented.[22] Joel himself identified Michael as
a rival in a poem from *The Glory Hole*:

[20] Letter, April 7, 1984.
[21] Arthur Miller, *Death of a Salesman* (New York: Viking,
1949), 16. For other themes in Miller, see **Gas** ("I suddenly couldn't drive any more" [13]) and **Time travel**
("I don't remember the last five minutes" [13]).
[22] Gale, e-mail to me, November 4, 2002. Gale felt herself drawn into this competition, where she was pitted
against Michael's wife.

I am in every way your brother.
 The womb you stretched before me
 led me into this world
 and together we grew
 in love and constant contention.

The world that bore us
 is the object of our greatest jealousies;
 her favor is claimed by us both.
 Our father, who gave us the freedom
 we realized in the land we call our home,
 watches and judges our growth,
 ready to snatch this gift
 from our hands
 if he deems us undeserving.

We are in every way brothers:
 Let us have our fights and arguments;
 And let us always have our love.

No one will mistake this for Whitman, but it does lay out the family romance on a grand terrain in the classic American way.[23] Joel's mother is the bountiful continent, spouse to a founding father, his gift of freedom not quite an inalienable right. The patriarch is less James Madison than Isaac; the siblings are biblical, Jacob and Esau in contention for a blessing only one can have.

Many of the poems in *The Glory Hole* are exercises in sarcastic scatology, but in this one the sentiment is refreshingly direct: Michael was someone with whom Joel wished to share love. In light of their future relations, the wish seems wishful thinking indeed, and the notion of a contest over the country's bounty a laughable misassessment of the brothers' relative chances.

[23] One of Joel's courses at Berkeley was taught by Henry Nash Smith, the "grand old man," author of *Virgin Land: The American West as Symbol and Myth* (Cambridge: Harvard University Press, 1950).

Death wish. "No one kills himself who did not want to kill another or, at least, wish death to another."[24] Less than a year after his mother's death, Joel gave a detailed account of a dream in which Michael too had died.[25] Perhaps that was a step in his preparations.

[24] Wilhelm Stekel, quoted in Alfred Adler et al., *On Suicide: With Particular Reference to Suicide among Young Students*, ed. Paul Friedman (New York: International Universities Press, 1967), 22.

[25] Letter, March 2, 1976. "I dreamt that my brother died and I spent the entire dream wandering over, around and through a perfectly hideous mountain of gothic architectural doodaddery adjacent to an assumably interminable pair of railroad tracks, crying, wailing, and generally making a great show of my grief."

Deference. A fatal politeness. Richard deferred to Joel; I deferred to Richard. I suspected Joel's gifts foretold some dark future. But in the end, I deferred to Richard's judgment and greater intimacy, and he deferred to faith in Joel's abhorrence of giving a friend this poison. But to make ready, he had to give it: "I've expressed my concern repeatedly, that I might be returning things that are gifts from you, but I'm going to expect you to receive them as proof of how much I've liked them. Ah, what a weight of guilt I feel being lifted from my weakening, bent shoulders."[26]

[26] Last letter to Richard, October 22, 1995.

Diabetes. A bounding horizon of Joel's life. He developed diabetes before he was out of elementary school, and he was not a cautious manager of his condition who lived a nearly normal life, the cheerful self-helper of pop psycho-think.

I asked Gale how Joel's diabetes affected him. She believed that "growing up diabetic in that particular Jewish family" may have been at the root of Joel's difficulties. "Remember," she wrote, that "as difficult as diabetes remains today, in those days it was almost medieval. Joel would talk about how his grandmother tested her urine by tasting it. And when he was small, they used glass syringes for him and sharpened the needles for reuse."[27]

Joel did not make a big thing out of eating, his need for certain foods in regulated amounts at regular intervals. To the contrary. He wanted not to think about it, to be or appear normal. Gale wrote:

> This led to some problems between him and me since, when we moved in together, I knew next to nothing about diabetes. He was very brittle in those days, and had many seizures linked to low blood sugar. Through trial and error

[27] Gale, e-mail to me,
November 4, 2002.

I learned to recognize warning signs and try to stop his sugar going lower, but he would often refuse to cooperate at that point. I remember once, we were with Richard, driving along the coast, and the car broke down. It was late afternoon. Joel thought nothing of it. I said something about needing to find some food for him soon. Richard walked or hitched somewhere and came back with something for him to eat. I don't think Joel would have ever mentioned that he needed to eat.

For Joel, every day had one beginning: rise early, inject himself, eat. If he waited too long, disaster. Richard saw it happen in the bad year of 1975. Dividing from Gale, Joel came down from Santa Barbara to stay for a few weeks with Richard in his rented duplex in Sherman Oaks. He slept on a foldout bed in the living room, and perhaps because he did not wish to occupy the one bathroom, or perhaps out of a distaste for concealment, or perhaps out of his mood of regret, he injected himself in plain sight, and Richard saw it happen.

One morning, late to rise, slow to move, Joel sat on the bed in his underwear, preparing his kit, facing the kitchen, where Richard was getting a breakfast together. They chatted around the corner, out of sight, and then Joel stopped chatting. When Richard came to see what was happening, Joel was in hypoglycemic seizure. The syringe had fallen to his side, used or unused, and Joel, still upright on the edge of the bed, spasmed like a damaged fish, spittle in the corners of his mouth.

"What should I do?" Richard shouted, pointlessly. "What should I do?" In a few moments the jerking ceased, the body slumped heavily, and Richard held him from the floor. Stricken, he phoned Joel's parents. His father answered, asked if Joel had taken insulin, said to give some fruit juice, said he would call an ambulance. He was remarkably calm, his voice resonant and smooth, reassuring. Later, mentioning the fear he had heard over the phone, he apologized on Joel's behalf for his failure to prepare Richard for such emergencies.

There was another episode that year as the two were driving in the Valley. Recognizing that his blood sugar was running out, Joel stopped his vw wagon at a supermarket to buy a candy bar. Inside he picked out his favorite Snickers and stood in line, while Richard headed back into the store to fetch a few staples. A minute later he heard over the PA an alarmed voice calling the manager to the front. Richard himself ran and found Joel on the floor in the aisle between the big front windows and the cash registers, unconscious, head cradled by a checkout clerk. He'd not gotten through the line in time, nor in his clouded state had sense enough to take some bites of the candy before paying.

"He's a diabetic. He needs juice, grapefruit juice!" Richard said forcefully. The clerk ran for it, and Richard, crooking Joel's neck, poured a little from the plastic bottle between his pursed lips. The excess ran down into the coarse dark hair at the back of his neck. It was a magic elixir, and in a few moments Joel roused and was able to stand, hold Richard's arm, and exit. The store manager was relieved to have the ugly scene done with. Richard got Joel into the car, felt its light gearshift for the first time, and drove Joel, nauseous and riven with headache, to his parents' house for care.

Richard came to feel a steady dread of more such incidents. In time, like Gale, he learned to recognize hypoglycemic signs in Joel: vagueness of thought, inability to make sense, an inclination of the head and wipe of the forehead while pausing to think, helplessly. By the time they lived together in San Francisco, he knew enough to encourage Joel to take food or to insist, against his thickening mind, that he must drink juice *now*.

But Richard also got angry over his dread. It boiled up one day when they were crossing the Bay Bridge. It was not a spot where one could get food, and the moment was right for a speech he had been rehearsing. He spoke of his fear and of Joel's failing to be prepared. The trick was to sound self-interested while passing a burden of guilt, undermining Joel's carelessness by turning care for himself, which Joel would resist, into concern for Richard. The little speech worked, and Joel began to carry quick forms of sugar with him in the car.

There were no more hypoglycemic reactions that I know of until a very bad one in October 1988, when no one was there to help.

> Two weeks ago, a Friday morning, I went to work with my leg hurting. By the time I arrived at the school, my leg was hurting very badly. I apologized to the principal's secretary and managed, in great pain, to drive to the Kaiser hospital, blessedly nearby. I went to the Emergency section and got to see a doctor fairly quickly. He said it was a problem with the sciatic nerve, expressed sincere sympathy, and gave me two prescriptions. Two problems occurred to me. First, I knew I could not take the pills first, then drive, so I wondered how I was going to get home. Second, I was concerned about the safety of my taking narcotics. I really pressed the doctor to consider the fact that I'm using insulin and living alone, but the doctor insisted there was nothing to worry about.

Was the doctor unworried because the initial dosage was not going to knock Joel out?

> Okay. So, I got the prescriptions—and if I'd been able to think a little bit more clearly, I would have taken them to

Walgreens and saved myself a fortune: the codeine alone cost $25! Then I forced myself into the car and, sweating and gnashing my teeth, somehow survived the trip home. Now I was supposed to take the pills and lie down. I couldn't lie down. I tried, but it just hurt unbearably. After a couple of hours had passed, I called the doctor and begged for a suggestion; he explained that there was nothing more that could be done, but I might try lying on my stomach—something I'd not tried because I'd been told to lie flat on my back—and take another couple pills.

I wonder if the doctor by this point had forgotten that Joel was using insulin and living alone.

The pain continued undiminished, and I kept trying and failing to lie down for another two hours. Now the pills really kicked in. The pain was still there, but I was finding it more and more difficult to remain standing: I kept falling asleep. At last, I found that I could lie on my stomach, and I was out like a light. Really out. Several hours later— or in diabetic terms—a couple of missed meals later—I returned to semi-consciousness, and was really hypoglycemic. I was in big trouble. Thinking and coordinating muscles is a major problem during a hypoglycemic episode; with the sciatic nerve problem, I found that I was nearly unable to move. I struggled for three hours to move three feet to the telephone, screaming for help between pushes. Finally, my hand found the phone cord, I somehow pulled the phone to a position that would allow me to press the buttons, and I struggled blindly—I couldn't maneuver the phone so I might see it, and it was getting dark, anyway— to get the operator. I finally did, but then I had to struggle to form noises recognizable as my name and address. I failed a couple of times, but finally got the operator and my message together, and the firemen and the ambulance guys arrived soon after.

How did the paramedics get into his apartment? They must have broken through two doors, the entrance from the street into the garage, and the entrance to the apartment itself. For Joel had sent no key.

Disposition of the body. When passengers are lost at sea, survivors pray for recovery of the bodies. The passengers are lost, but relatives want to know where the ship went down; they need to reconstruct events, even if that reconstruction cannot be certain. They speak of waiting forever for their lost loved ones to return. If they don't know the details of death and haven't recovered the remains, they can't relinquish the hope that the dead may resurface. They speak of closure, their need to pick up the mantle of living. There is a difference in feeling and meaning between *lost at sea* and *buried at sea*. The former implies a quarrel with death that can't be won; the latter suggests acceptance and a process completed. Grief for soldiers missing in action, whose bodies are never recovered, cannot be laid to rest. A son's grave at Arlington is, by contrast to this unfinished death, comforting.

In the rituals of mourning, we substitute a final resting place, even one so unmarked as the sea, for the actual place of death. We do so to write over the terrible image of trauma. Substitution of place is our profound device in death and its aftermath. The image of final burial comforts us because we, the survivors, compose it. It is authored rather than thrust upon us, already engraved. Choice of the place and manner of burial gains us composure against the suddenness of tragedy. Those who were lost are no longer lost: they are laid to rest. Meanwhile, the rituals of cremation purify the image of autopsy. The work of mourning is incomplete without a final substitution ("So Lycidus, sunk low, but mounted high").

About death we say that closure is necessary. If questions about cause or manner exist, answers must be found. Yet suicide frustrates causal explanations. We perform autopsy—the clinical inspection of the body—to ascertain the physiological cause of death. Birth certificates note the time we come into the world, and death certificates note the time we depart, sometimes with a false exactitude. But dates and times, places and paths—are these the answers we seek?

Joel left no instructions for the disposition of his body. He knew quite well that's the business of survivors. His father thought the Rose Garden a good match, I'm sure. It's true that Joel loved roses, loved their difficulty. But his love was intimate, for that which grew in his backyard, climbing a seasoned trellis, not an orchestrated display. Woodlawn must be an orderly place, with rows of rose arbors, a fountain from which no water springs, and emptiness. There death is sanitized, corporately managed. The Rose Garden at Woodlawn may have comforted Joel's father, but it does not console me. For me he is lost at sea.

Disposition of the weapon. What do the police do with the guns they collect from the public? Guns used as evidence in a trial, once they have confessed their role, are added temporarily to a police stockpile, where they fall mute to the deeds they've committed, the particularity of their offense erased in a warehouse of weapons.

Under California law the police can arrange to have a gun destroyed. Some guns are chopped into scrap metal and sold by the pound, while others are liquefied at foundries. Tamco Steel in Rancho Cucamonga melts and recycles weapons as rebar that is used to repair freeways and bridges (see **Golden Gate**).[28]

A legal gun may be auctioned by the police—perhaps its fate if it has a genealogy, is a family heirloom, a museum piece, a collector's fine item. But who would want a gun with a history of suicide, like a house in which a tragedy has occurred, serviceable in every way, yet empty it sits, unpurchased except by newcomers to town or a speculator who cares nothing about history. Who would want Joel's .38? "We used to have a pawn shop here that had auctions of guns they bought off some west coast police dept's. Some were fine guns. . . . I almost bought one with some rusty blotches on the barrel until someone told me it was a suicide gun."[29]

[28] Gary Friedman, "Confiscated Weapons to Be Melted into Rebar," *Los Angeles Times*, July 26, 2010.

[29] Panther22, message-board post, October 15, 2008, http://www.thehighroad.org.

Distance learning. Joel spent his last high school days not in class but roaming widely in his father's white Corvair, with forays out into the Mojave.

Domestic past. You entered the apartment through a spacious garage; his neighbor, Chuck, lived in the house above, to which the apartment had been added on. All of it formed a little complex. Traversing the garage, you went through a small doorway at the rear into the apartment proper, with the bathroom door right in front of the entry. Turning left, you moved into the combined kitchen and living room, the latter of which was carpeted and in which Joel slept on a fold-up couch-bed. Near the refrigerator in the kitchen was the doorway to a second room, much of it occupied with his harpsichord and shelves for his books. The walls were mostly bare and light-colored to keep the room bright on San Francisco's cloudy days. From this second room you had access to the backyard, a small garden porch, and Joel's roses. The yard, his to use exclusively, was about the size of his apartment, if you don't include the garage in the calculations.

Dream. If I made up a dream: Joel was following me in his car. We played all kinds of road games. I tried to trick and lose him, racing over a bridge, only to find his headlights waiting for me.

Eagle. The river house is made much of glass, and I often catch
something in my eye outside the windows and run for my binoculars. By the time I stop fumbling and manage to remove
them from their cozy case, get the two caps off the eyepieces,
and fit them to my eyes, I've lost whatever I fleetingly saw.
Usually birds are on the move; they don't linger as subjects of
portraiture, and I have only seconds to see them.

But sometimes the great birds of prey will survey the scene
from their perch for long enough that I can train my glass on
them. I have watched a hawk remain motionless for five minutes, except for rotating his head in an occasional flick.

From my study I see the river through a maze of trees. Once,
looking up from my computer, I saw a dark, large shape land
on a tree across the river downstream from us. I could see the
branch bounce with the weight and knew it was a large bird
come down. But it was too far away and too obscured by trees
for me to see what kind of bird it was. I wanted to name it, and
I ran for the binoculars. By the time I got them out, the bird
had moved on. Still scanning the area, I spotted it straddling a
branch in another tree closer to me. A bald eagle.

The first time you see a bald eagle, you are stunned by
its size. This one was so large that its purchase upon the
branch of the robust fir was precarious. It didn't stay long but

hop-scotched its stellar way from tree to tree up the corridor of the river in a midnight zigzag of black and white until it straightened out and flew up the center of the stream and out of sight. I ran out onto the balcony and tried to follow its white-tipped head as far as I could, ecstatic with the sighting of the eagle just passing through on its way to somewhere else.

Egg coddler.

Something with
a surprise inside.
See **Last words to me**.

As he was ridding his apartment of his last possessions,
Joel may have found the egg coddler languishing way back
on a high shelf, coated in dust. Sweeping for whatever items
remained, he stood on a chair, reached as far back as he could,
and felt its cold sides. He stuffed the proceeds of the sale of his
car into the egg coddler and sent it to me. It was a convenient
container, the right size for a wad of bills. Perhaps he thought,
wryly, *I'll send Marcia a nest egg*.

I don't know the story behind the egg coddler, its origins. I
can't know the place of this object in Joel's life, what significance, if any, it had. I'd like to think he used the coddler; that's
a story I tell myself, though he didn't use it every day. He lived
alone, and a coddler for one would have suited him. I can see
him simmering an egg from time to time, unscrewing the
lid, tapping the sides with his spoon to help the egg slide out
onto his toast. The egg would jiggle as it slithered out, almost
jellied. He'd cut it up, breaking the yolk so it would run onto
his thin wheat toast. He was a fastidious eater. Living alone,
with little to attend to, he ruminated on the details of his daily

life—his meals, the purchase of groceries, his weight. He opened his cupboard, reaching behind his saucers, and lifted the coddler out of its appointed spot, happily noting its solitary swallow in flight, its fit in his grip. After cooking and eating his egg, he held the empty coddler in his hand, still warm as a living thing.

But did he use it? I don't know that. Maybe the coddler sat untouched from the time it entered his apartment (Richard says he never knew Joel to eat a coddled egg). I've looked for telltale signs, but my findings are inconclusive. On the outside the coddler shows no chips, fractures, discolorations, or other signs of wear. When I screw off the lid and peer inside, a few flecks the color of egg yolk show in contrast to the creamy china. Are these flecks the discoloration that appears in old objects that have been stored unused? To know, I'd have to send the coddler to a lab, subject it to a battery of scientific tests and analysis, like Joel's body in autopsy.

What I can know is that he chose the egg coddler to transport the thousand dollars to me and that its final use was not its original purpose. Joel subverted its purpose and used it to bring a surprise to me, the surprise of money—and the surprise of his death. As the new owner, as the designated recipient of the egg coddler, I sustain Joel's practice, not using the coddler for its purpose of cooking eggs. Instead, the coddler, in the Swallow pattern, sits on a bookshelf in my study, in limbo and in memoriam, at the stark forefront of my vision if I swivel my chair to pick up a book. Floating flowers swirl in mauve and yellow, a few purple petals among green leaves, more like tendrils, and a single yellow bird, its wings tinged black and suspended to the side of the flowers on a cream-colored background. Its wings hang in the air like a set of floating jaws.

When I look at the coddler, I think of the tangle of his death, think that I won't ever know what he felt or intended for me, won't understand my role in his life or his death, what purpose I served in his story. Emotional turmoil swoops down and seizes me like the swallow. Move on, I say to myself, get a grip. And I want to move on, but there's always a new wrinkle in this surviving business: the dead pop up in my dreams, playing on their resemblance to a living person. I bestow upon the coddler more significance than it likely had in life. I watch a drama, a tiny theater where plays a tragedy that begins and ends differently each time it is performed on my shelf.

Endings. The novelist creates the beginning and discovers where she is going as the plot unfolds. Her characters know still less than she does and suffer the hurts and shames of benightment (see **Role**). But I, a secretary, know where all the plot lines end.

English 1B. She had gone underground, and Joel could no longer be "the apple of his mom's eye, abnormally so," as Gale put it.[30] Gale's familiar expression, *the apple of her eye*, was made familiar by the King James Bible,[31] which uses it in several verses to translate a Hebrew idiom that more literally means "little man of the eye," the reflection of another person in the pupil. It is a perfect term, birthed by the lady luck of language, for the maternal outlook on the son. Her view is not literal, as the world sees him, an ordinary child; it metaphorizes the boy, transforming him into the fruit of her womb.

Joel must have considered what part he, the little man, had played in his mother's suicide. She died from lack of love, after all, and he doubted his power to love, to relieve her deficiency. But he did not speak of it, and there were no more overt mentions of her after English 1A. She had gone underground, to a distinct realm, and his references were now oblique, as if the line between the quick and the dead were a trick of language, to be traversed by substitution and other symbolic means.

Now the boy had to metaphorize the mother, to descry her through our mortal scope of words.

[30] Gale, e-mail to me, November 4, 2002.
[31] Deut. 32:10 and elsewhere.

Epictetus. Greek Stoic philosopher, circa AD 55–135. He commended suicide as the right path in the face of irremediable suffering, represented by an image of smoke:

> Has someone made smoke in the house? If it is moderate, I will stay; if too much, I go outside. For you must always remember and hold fast to this, that the door is open.

> If I am so wretched, death is my haven. This is the haven of everyone, death, this is our refuge. That is why nothing that befalls us in life is difficult. Whenever you wish you can exit and no longer be troubled by smoke.

> Remember that the door is open. Do not be more cowardly than children, but just as they say, when the game no longer pleases them, "I will play no more," you too, when things seem that way to you, should merely say, "I will play no more," and so depart; but if you stay, stop moaning.[32]

Fair enough. I only ask: What if I have set myself on fire? See **Method.**

[32] The Discourses of Epictetus, ed. Christopher Gill, translation revised by Robin Hard (London: J. M. Dent, 1995), 1.25.18, 4.10.27, 1.24.20.

Esse est percipi. To be is to be perceived. "The man who desires to cease to be must cease to be perceived. If being is being perceived, to cease being is to cease to be perceived."[33]

It is difficult enough to enter another person's life when both parties are willing to find the crossing points between two wills, minds, and hearts. Joel made the crossing impossible, destroying the bridges. He underwent a long self-annihilation inside a solitary apartment, locking the door behind him. He lived with an eye fixed on departure, with ties so tenuous they could be snapped without anyone's knowing till after the last act in the last place, his role in others' lives so light that when he removed himself from it, his weightless absence left no ripple.

[33] Samuel Beckett quoted in Barney Rosset, "Beginning to End: Publishing and Producing Beckett," in *A Companion to Samuel Beckett*, ed. S. E. Gontarski (Malden, Mass.: Wiley-Blackwell, 2010), 55.

Eulogy. Suicide deprives survivors of the sanctioned rituals of burial and mourning. Joel's suicide destroyed ritual and gave us no hold with which to brace ourselves. In a funeral or memorial service, a tribute is delivered to the dead by ministers, friends, and family. Eulogies pay respect, in summation of a life lived. The narrative of death is crucial to interpretation of the life, integral to the story survivors tell.

Suicide turns eulogy inside out, writing over the life, substituting for what might have been said by others a text so short it consists only of the author's signature. It wrenches the conventions of consolation, the rituals of grieving, from persons left behind. Joel's act drained the life from our memories of what we were and who he was. A life burned away deliberately—what can be made from such a life and such a death?

Failure. "To be an artist is to fail, as no other dare fail, that failure is his world and the shrink from it desertion, art and craft, good housekeeping, living."[34]

[34] Samuel Beckett, *Disjecta: Miscellaneous Writings and a Dramatic Fragment* (New York: Grove, 1984), 145. I have been tempted to fill out the clotted grammar here with some bracketed interpolations, but faith in Beckett is always repaid.

Fast car. The two necessary facts to know about Joel and automobiles are

1. He never drove a new, perfectly functioning, shock-absorbers-intact, unrusted, door-closing, fast-accelerating car.

2. He never drove a car that wasn't subsidized or previously owned by his father.

Joel was always in a state of anxiety about his car's performance. Would it start? Would the brakes bring him to a stop on the hills of San Francisco? Was air escaping from the tires? Was the car leaking oil or overheating? Were the taillights working? Doors didn't shut properly; broken turn signals necessitated frantic hand signals; iffy starter motors meant parking with the front end of the car aiming downhill to get a running jump. The windshield wipers smeared rain into a thick coat across the window. No heat, no defrost, no acceleration.

Joel was close-mouthed about many of his problems. Instead he talked about the troubles he was experiencing with his car:

[35] Letter, February 16, 1983. Skyline is a school in South San Francisco.

"Yesterday, my brakes were feeling a bit odd and by the time I got back from Skyline, the right front brake was smoking."[35]

On one visit to San Francisco, six months pregnant, I was forced to wait on the sidewalk, then run downhill and jump into a car—when the engine caught—that jounced and bottomed out over the cable car tracks because the shocks were shot, then wait again while Joel stopped to check the air in the tires. In the backseat I was poised for disaster, wondering at the entrance to the freeway if we'd make it up the ramp, wondering whether we'd stop at the red light at the foot of the hill or sail through Fisherman's Wharf. Indeed, the brakes were especially worrisome. Even after they were supposedly repaired, Joel wrote: "My car was released into my custody once more. Bail was $100. The mechanic said, 'You'll be able to drive it till it falls apart.' Tautological, but sinister. Fact is, the brakes are really terrible now and I dread having to apply them: the car goes in all different directions."[36]

He sputtered from one car to the next, taping the upholstery together, driving nowhere far for fear he wouldn't make it back. Breakdowns, reports of the repairs needed, what he'd have to give up to finance those repairs—his letters were full of these accountings. Car woes attached to descriptions of his depression and anger:

> I am depressed. In addition to many of the sources of
> depression inherent in the state of nature—the effort
> of breathing, the accumulation of fatty tissue, the need
> to trim fingernails—are the purely artificial agencies of
> garage mechanics, pharmacists, and grocery clerks, all

[36] Letter, February 23, 1983.

performing their black ministries against our happiness and well-being.

It is not fun being poverty-stricken and physically unimposing in America.

He didn't make job interviews because his car broke down; he blew interviews to which he arrived late and flustered because he had stopped for repairs. One such incident took place at Vacaville High School:

Because I'm not entirely stupid, it had occurred to me to rent a car for the trip, but I proved sufficiently stupid to have gone ahead and driven my vw.[37] After the first 15 minutes it had become necessary forcibly to hold the car in gear—after having ground it into gear with sweat and prayers—while steering and signaling turns with the other. Slowing down meant multiple troubles: the brakes were very bad, causing the car to veer strongly to the left; downshifting was virtually impossible; and shifting back up was a great trial. My nerves were probably in a traumatized state soon after I left home. With my right arm frozen in defiance of the gear shift, my left in attendance upon the steering wheel, I was conscious of little else but the need to spot the Vacaville exit if it should ever appear, and the fact is that the highway is as good a metaphor for life as any, that there are many ways to exit, and that this was no time to develop a predilection for any particular one of them. . . . Somehow I made it to Vacaville. The car sounded like a rattling pail of nuts and bolts. I'd arrived early enough to ask the auto shop instructor to have a look and advise me of my chances of getting back to S.F. He

[37] This was the same vw that had broken down on the coast south of Santa Barbara (see **Diabetes**).

told me that the transmission wouldn't just freeze up, but it was likely something would burn out before I got home. So I decided to drive it back.

Joel didn't get the job.

His cars were castoffs from his father, Corvairs ("unsafe at any speed") and Pintos (of explosive gas tank fame), as if in flagrant defiance of Ralph Nader. Joel almost never mentioned a car problem without his father popping up: "Have I told you about the car my father decided it was time I bought? If not, I hope I thought I was being stoical or something."[38] And: "My father's pulled another car-oriented freaky."[39] The fragile VW that had moved my first pregnancy along Joel finally disposed of after wrestling an old Pinto from his father.

> I lost a day's work yesterday because my new old car's battery died. I guess I haven't explained the great car arrangement. It isn't something I really want to think about. Suffice it to say I've got the VW parked on the street and it is supposed to be turned into some cash in payment for the '71 Pinto I picked up from my father. To get my father to part with the Pinto—which he's driven twice—was a major undertaking; and he's still making me sweat over the disposition of the VW: he doesn't want me to get less for it than it's worth. My father has an irrational side that somehow or other finds my soft parts and leaves them covered with stinging, bloody abrasions.[40]

His last car-related narrative was written in the all-important month April 1995, when he reached a turning point in his struggle to live.

[38] Letter, August 1988.
[39] Letter, May 1983.
[40] Letter, October 1984.

I awoke with the feeling that I needed to move on what I believed (knew) to be a problem with my car's camshaft, and drove down to the garage that's been doing all my car work for the past 10+ years. First, they confirmed my suspicions and my judgment that I ought not to put the work off till summer, and second, they gave me an estimate . . . which was, in itself, horrible enough; but they also attached a verbal rider about what would happen in terms of parts and labor if there'd been collateral damage to the valves. As always, I went home, walked around for an hour frantically weighing repair alternatives (none), financial alternatives (substitute teach? summer employment? cancel the cable service and stop eating?), and scheduling alternatives (on what days would the cancellation of my home teaching appointments least impact my students' progress? on what days would the cancellation least impact my students' parents' consciousness?), and then, putting aside my manic reflections, called and made an appointment for next Wednesday. If all goes well, the job can be done in one day. Just once, I'd like the attendant Fates to pass up an opportunity to show me the risks of living on the financial edge. . . . You don't have these worries: in time of need, you can sell your children.[41]

These stories make all the more improbable the appearance of his Escort wagon in our driveway on that October afternoon.

[41] Letter, April 21, 1995.

Figurines (1). I am not a collector. When I was seven or eight years old, Aunt Virgie began to give me horse figurines for Christmas and birthdays, knowing that I loved real horses. Other aunts and uncles followed suit, and soon the shelves in my bedroom held a herd of carved wood ponies and plastic stallions. But I wanted horses in the flesh. I liked my horses outside in pastures, in well-kept stables that smelled thick with hay, horses scratching their behinds on the doors of stalls.[42] If I couldn't look at the sheen of a living flank or muzzle, I'd have nothing—certainly not the matte plastic of these substitutes. I did not want to bring the noble animals home, to shrink them down so they would fit through the door, to freeze them in one stationary pose, rearing up and pawing an air they could not feel.

As soon as propriety allowed, I gave the figurines to my niece, who, lacking an engagement with the living creature, cared for them and

[42] "I first saw him on my thirteenth birthday. My parents drove me through the snow to the stable. A brass plate on his stall read ALERT INDIAN in large letters. When Miss Reba opened his stall, snow was falling outside the window behind him, and the straw was fresh and golden and piled thickly. Standing in the straw was sixteen hands of blackness. When the door slid open, every inch of him was startled. His muscles tensed from his head all along his back to the flicking tail. His neck was arched and tight, his eyes widened and white, his head high and turned toward me. It was finely shaped, intelligent, watchful. His muzzle was a soft, smooth black. He exceeded my thought of what a horse could be" (Marcia Aldrich, "Ingenuity," in *Girl Rearing* [New York: Norton, 1998], 99).

displayed them proudly. Sometimes on a visit, entering her room I felt a cold breeze, a shivering along my spine, at the sight of a horse mounted on a shelf.

I have never wanted to collect, am compelled to minimize my attachments, to essentialize. I tell myself this is part of my philosophy of living: to compact all things into myself. As a rule I don't keep letters, cards, drafts, backup copies, paper trails, as most writers I know do. One friend saved every word I had written her since we were in college, arranging the corpus in color-coded folders. She thought this would please me, attest to her belief that we would be famous. I informed her that I had not kept her letters and wished she'd destroy mine. She would not, and I stopped writing her.

During one period of my life I kept letters in an old trunk. Then one summer when it had filled I burned them in the driveway. This impulse to destroy was a response to pain, of course, for some of the letters came from a man whose affections I no longer held. To burn his love letters was the only act left to me: if I couldn't have him, I didn't want his haunting words. With some emotions, there is no substitute for *Good riddance*.

Perhaps this was Joel's feeling in his final stage. Until the very end of his life he kept everything. His instincts and training made it impossible for him to throw away so much as a cheap lapel button with a silly slogan. He wore shirts until they were threadbare and buttonless and then wore them more. But at the end, what thing could he keep, what might he collect, that would keep him alive? It is impossible to collect health or happiness, isn't it? Objects that spoke of a life worth living would have been mere signs of it, like tiny horses rearing on a windowsill.

Figurines (2). I would not be writing this if Joel were alive. There would be no need. It is the traverser of the underworld who requires a companion-guide. Even the great organ of elegy can only substitute a poetic creation for the person who died.

Finality. We do our best to avoid it, defy it. We dislike good-byes, departures, breakups, losses of memory, exile, divorce, aging, and death. Suicide is final. You cannot take back what was said or done, can no longer contemplate some long-desired but never-achieved understanding or forgiveness. See **Gun**.

Fleck. A crack in the glass of Joel's life so fine we couldn't see it, a dark fleck, the speck that contained an epic treatise on shattering.

Gale. The one woman. Joel met her at the University of Utah (see **Higher education**); they began living together in 1970 and moved to Santa Barbara in 1973. In July 1974 she planned a trip alone to Europe, which Joel (perhaps believing her travel a temporary separation) described in mild terms: "She's planning a sort of voyage of discovery, hoping to relieve herself of certain doubts she has about the authenticity of her self. This, of course, is expressed in my own terms; Gale simply wishes to try being on her own—something she has never really been."[43] Of her motivations for this separation Gale herself said, "The dreams I thought we shared weren't there anymore. I was determined to go back to school, to travel, to live frivolously. He was paying bills and talking of buying cars."[44]

Toward the end of the year, he knew it was over (see **Young manhood**), and he left Santa Barbara to look for work in L.A.

[43] Letter, July 13, 1974.
[44] Gale, e-mail to me, October 30, 2002.

Garage sale. The project of his last months was to get rid of all that he had accumulated. Joel prepared his own death by eradicating traces of his life. He emptied his apartment with precision and care, leaving the minimum to be faced by survivors.

With less intimate items he might have had a garage sale or giveaway, complete with flyer: *Come Get the Last Remains*. Posters, plates, cups, pans, spices, books, magazines, typewriters, mattress, sheets, pillows, blankets, clothes, tables, chairs, posters, record albums, lamps, tapes, clocks, radios, toaster, shoes, pottery, teas, nail clippers, shower curtain, toothbrushes, coffee pot, mugs, cheese grater, vacuum cleaner, knives, can opener, sleeping bag, Comet, broom, magnets, detergents, scrub brush, toilet bowl cleaner, mouthwash, dental floss, suitcases, book bag, soap, shampoo, comb, trash cans, pencils, vinegar, socks, baking powder, sugar, instruction manuals, rose fertilizer, shovels, dictionaries, videos, plants, vases, scissors, ironing board, iron. Imagine.

All was threadbare, had come to him used, or was so cheaply made that in no time it already looked worn, suitable for the homeless. His possessions were the sort no one wanted in the first place, hand-me-downs, discards from his father's household, purchased at garage sales, thrift shops, inherited from his dead neighbor, or picked up curbside. They had no monetary value, yet even a meager life must be disposed of. Let those who came to a giveaway paw through the kitchen equipment, his bath mat and towels. He did not care. Let someone snatch up a single item eagerly. Let her finger a plate, a bottle opener, and decide the price—next to nothing, or nothing.

Gas. Painting by Edward Hopper from 1940, depicting a man standing near gas pumps, in the lonely isolation typical of Hopper. The man might be straightening the area, checking supplies of motor oil. Or maybe he's filling himself up with gas—a transfusion of energy he needs, because he looks bent and tired.

Inspired by his long-term struggles to maintain a reliable means of transportation (see **Fast car**), I think of Joel when I look at this painting. He didn't work at a gas station or live on a lonesome road, but alone in a dark apartment, sitting on his foldout bed with a book before him or standing at a window that looked onto a plot of roses shrouded in San Francisco mist. Older, tired, attending. Or standing at an erased blackboard in one of the classrooms he temporarily occupied. He's trying to keep the internal fires burning against the wall of darkness pressing in. He is attending to the small tasks of the living, until he just runs out of gas.

Gender gap. Men are more likely than women to choose guns to achieve the desired outcome, for reasons that are studied and speculated on by experts. Some suggest that women dislike a technique that results in disfigurement; others believe that women in death are like women in life, less violent. Still others suggest that women may be more tentative in their approach, choosing an option that might lead to survival.

Gifts. Was Joel hoping we would see through his deceptions? Suicide textbooks inform us that "suicidal behavior is a form of communication in which the person is expressing in a desperate and dangerous way his feelings about himself, the situation in which he feels enmeshed, and his need for some kind of attention and help."[45] The textbooks say the presuicide's communication is not always expressed verbally. It may take an indirect form, "as in the preparation for permanent absence by giving away treasured possessions."[46]

In the months before his suicide, we were the recipients of objects Joel no longer wanted. Never one to throw things away, he shepherded his treasured possessions eastward to our home. He was simplifying his life—that's how he explained his divestiture, and Richard believed the lies he was told. On his last visit, having already shipped his telescope, Joel delivered to us his microscope, binoculars, computer, tools, and books. Our children, we all believed, were of an age when they would benefit from looking far and looking near.

[45] Edwin S. Shneidman, ed., *Essays in Self-Destruction* (New York: Science House, 1967), 384.

[46] Shneidman, *Essays in Self-Destruction*, 385.

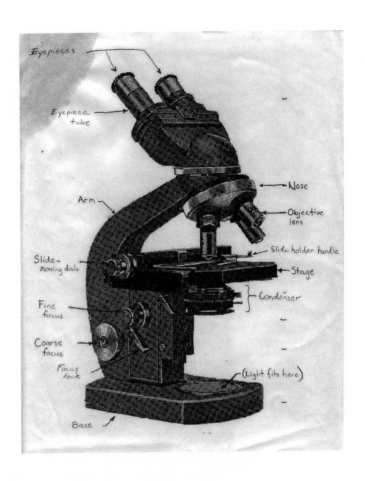

Eyepieces

Eyepiece tube

Arm

Slide-moving dials

Fine focus

Coarse focus

Focus lock

Base

Nose

Objective lens

Slide holder handle

Stage

Condenser

(Light fits here)

Later we saw that he was giving us more than his things—
that some indestructible property was being passed along.

Now, after his death, the items he gave us lie under a dark
burden. We cannot peel from them his deception in bestow-
ing them. In German *der Gift* means poison, the venom of the
snake.

The Glory Hole. A pamphlet of his poems that Joel, shortly after quitting high school, typed up on heavyweight paper and assembled between pasteboard covers with brass clips. Some of the poems he sent to Karl Shapiro, respecting his powers of assessment. So far as I know, the quondam editor of *Poetry* and *Prairie Schooner*, the man who said, "Suicide has cause,"[47] made no reply.

[47] Karl Shapiro, "Auto Wreck," in *Selected Poems*, ed. John Updike (New York: Library of America, 2003), 2.

Golden Gate. A place of many suicides. Such a spot seizes the imagination and becomes a "suicide magnet."[48] Waterloo Bridge in London, the Sussex Cliffs on the English coast, the Eiffel Tower, the forest called Jukai at the foot of Mount Fuji, Mount Mihara on the Japanese island Oshima, the Golden Gate Bridge, burnished in accounts replete with symbolism and suggestion, allure new pilgrims to follow those who have gone before. Here the naked act is dressed in ritual, sanctioned by tradition, sanctified by a community of the like-minded. One survivor of his leap from the Golden Gate said, "There is a kind of form to it, a certain grace and beauty."[49]

M. F. K. Fisher finds a "collection of spirit strength or power or love in these places that says, no, or yes, or now."[50] She believes there should be a sanctioned spot where one can go to one's death. Such is the Golden Gate Bridge, a structural marvel and shrine where people still jump in impressive numbers. See **Spectacular suicide.**

[48] Kay Redfield Jamison, *Night Falls Fast* (New York: Vintage, 2000), 146.

[49] Jamison, *Night Falls Fast*, 149.

[50] M. F. K. Fisher, "Those Who Must Jump," in *Telling Stories*, ed. Joyce Carol Oates (New York: Norton, 1998), 278.

Gun. In his left hand—he was left-handed—a .38 caliber revolver, with a five-round cylinder. Guns are used in 60 percent of all suicides in the United States. A gunshot is the most effective method, the most lethal, the most irreversible. Once the trigger is pulled, there are no second thoughts, unlike gas in an oven or pills.

Joel throughout his life had no gun and no interest in guns. He must have investigated possible methods, settled on a gunshot, and purchased a device for that purpose. He never bought a consumer good without first researching the product, I'm sure. He would have studied the effects when a gun is fired. Different calibers have different muzzle velocities. For his purposes, a low muzzle velocity was best, because he would not want the bullet to go straight through him. In this he planned well.

In his call to us (see **Thanksgiving**), Joel's father keened about the gun, shocked to know that his son owned one. How could a gun be a part of Joel's life, like bed and socks and books?

I have never held a gun in my hand. I've never purchased a gun magazine or entered the doors of a gun shop. I have never seen a gun lying in a drawer; no one I've ever been intimate with has owned a gun. I don't know how much guns cost or weigh. I don't know how the .38 fit Joel's hand, whether it dwarfed his hand or clicked into place naturally. I don't know if the trigger pulled stiffly, as a dry cork sticks in a wine bottle. I don't know how loud the gunshot was inside the bathroom, though I think the walls muffled the blast.

In my imagination the gun is huge, distorted surreally by my fear and horror, and Joel's body small.

The gun is just a detail in Joel's death moves. What does it matter now how he came to be in possession of it? What can't be traversed is the mystery, the gap between the gentle man we knew and the man who decided to use an enormity to kill himself.

Halloween. Time of year when people die. Ghosts hang from tree limbs, collide against the trunks, swing as if from the gallows. Cut pumpkins on stoops are drenched with rain; no candle will light tonight. During this holiday, Joel was busily emptying his apartment.

Harbor. In the following years, many women slept on the **bed of metamorphosis**. The bodies piled up. It moved to San Francisco, then from one apartment to another within the city. In that place of mists the blue plastic mattress, with its unearthly sheen, was cold even in summer, and Richard switched to a foam mattress—the mattress I would later sleep on. He added bricks at the corners to raise the frame off the ground. Over time the red ink on the plywood stained the foam, its misspelling preserved.

By then Richard and the bed had moved to Seattle, where we—Richard, the bed, and I—all met. When I visited him in his studio apartment for the first time, our relationship was conducted across the bed's broad expanse. You couldn't ignore it: when you walked through the front door, there it was, two feet to your right, with a narrow passage between frame and wall. On the opposite side ran another narrow passage between bed and the bank of windows looking out to the street. On my first visit, I perched on a radiator by the window, sipping a cup of tea, while Richard reclined on the bed. The next time I visited, he was folding laundry from a basket on the bed. We sprawled our bodies across the clean-smelling towels, socks, and folded white undershirts.

When Richard moved into my apartment, the bed came too, replacing the narrow one I had been sleeping on. My apartment had a large, proper bedroom, yet the bed, California king in dimensions, filled it. The bricks at the corners were unmoored and often shifted out from under the frame, jutting into my path so I could stub my toe while changing the sheets. Even with the bolster of bricks, the bed lay low to the ground.

Its history bothered me. Passed from man to man, the bed had given itself to a series of lovers who reclined in my imagination like empresses. At night I lay in the middle of something; relationships, failed or ephemeral, cast their shadows across the sheets. When I lay down on the bed, I lay down with others. When I was loving Richard, I was loving all the others who had lain on the bed. I was loving Joel, who was loving Richard; I was loving Gale, who was loving Joel, who was loving Richard. When I leaned back on the pillows, all those we had intimately known came to lie down beside me. When Richard joined me there and swept the hair from my forehead, he was sweeping the hair of every woman he'd known. The bed groaned, and I thought surely it would break. I did not want to lie down upon a bed so many had lain upon before me, but I did, for it could hold multitudes.

It was a good bed, the foam firm and wonderfully comfortable, ample enough to accommodate the children that issued from it, to hide cats in its folds, to sleep dogs peacefully at its foot. We had picnics and holidays on it, sailed ships across it. Life began on that bed, and the end of life was mourned there. Heavily pregnant, I would roll over the side to set my feet on the floor and pull myself up using a chair. The bed had nothing to grab hold of, nothing to hold onto, a massive raft afloat on the world's soul.

We slept on the bed of metamorphosis for sixteen years.

Both of our children were conceived on it, I nursed them there, they slept with us in it. It moved many times, from apartment to apartment, from house to house, and state to state. I threw myself in anger and despair upon it, I was colder than cold in it and hotter than hot, frosts covered me and fans blew over me naked on muggy summer nights. I heard the death throes of animals and the cries of newborn babies. From my pillows I saw a hawk perched at the window in December. I slept hugging its sides, and I knew its middle.

Heart. 245 grams.

Heron, doe, and fawns. We had no idea what we would see outside our windows at the river house. We knew we'd see the river, we knew we'd see trees, but we didn't know what lived in these trees, this river, what would pass through. Soon after moving in, standing at the kitchen sink washing dishes, I looked out the big bay window and spied a deer grazing in the wooded area on the other side of the river, nearly camouflaged in the tall autumnal grass. The deer munched on grasses in a calm, steady way and yet I felt compelled to watch. In this wooded area, away from houses, the deer seemed at ease. I watched her eat, focusing on the motion of her mouth chewing for thirty minutes.

This was the third time I'd reached for the binoculars in the six weeks we'd lived in our river house. The first time was to zoom in on what turned out to be a great blue heron balanced on a floating log in the middle of the river, near the banks directly behind our house. From the distance of our house and through our window, the heron looked chalky white but seemed too large for a white heron. Up close, through the eyes of the binoculars, I saw swatches of blue-gray streaks tufting into the milky blue that had looked like white chalk. I saw, too, how he was at himself cleaning, pecking at the parasites in his plumage.

I began to look for him regularly—standing in the shallows of the river, tucked into the banks—and when I didn't find him through my glass, I became concerned.

More recently a doe and her two fawns crossed the river and scrambled up the banks into our yard. They stayed a half hour and ate the hostas to the ground and much else. I let them. I could have walked out on the back balcony and disturbed them. But I had never before been so close to deer for so long. The doe was alert at all times, ears pricked at any sound or movement, absolutely still, still as a snake, standing outside my study windows in the woods. Her two fawns were less vigilant, relying on her for their watch, and free to scour the brush. Occasionally they looked to where I was, face obscured behind my binoculars. I couldn't tell if they could see me through the windows; I didn't see any signs that they could. I felt like a detective hired to sniff out adultery, the other woman, eavesdropping on the easy dinner banter of a husband and wife.

But all the analogies are wrong because they portray humans trespassing on humans. This was different; I was entering a different world, where I hadn't been invited.

Higher education. Joel, done with high school but lacking a
   diploma, dipped into community colleges. In the fall of 1967, he
   tried Los Angeles Valley College, where his mother worked in the
   admissions office. He viewed his classes with contempt. In a writing course he was supposed to compose an imaginary dialogue
   between two historical figures; they could have been Karl Marx
   and James Baldwin. In Joel's opinion, the two could never speak
   to one another. The assignment was the instructor's botch.

   Joel next tried Oakland's Merritt Junior College, living with
   Michael, who was attending Berkeley. Merritt was where Bobby
   Seale and Huey Newton had recently invented black campus
   consciousness. People were angry, Joel said, and every time
   you came to an intersection at the same time as a driver on the
   cross street, it was a political confrontation.

   Back in L.A. with his parents, Joel applied to and was
   rejected by Cal Lutheran and several other institutions because
   he had no high school diploma. But then came a significant
   turn. His uncle, who was on the faculty of the University of
   Utah, arranged to have Joel admitted there. In fall of 1969 he
   started at Utah, majoring in philosophy, residing in Ballif Hall,
   the dorm where Gale was also living. By fall of 1970, they had
   moved out of the dorm and were sharing an apartment.[51] Joel

[51] "We moved in together that fall, something that happened
   naturally and without a lot of discussion, and it was very good.
   We were good friends, had a social group we hung around with,
   mostly eggheads" (Gale, e-mail to me, October 30, 2002).

"began to struggle with school, incredible writer's block, excruciating."[52] By 1973 Gale was tired of Utah; they moved west, to Santa Barbara, and Joel began classes at UC Santa Barbara. There he floundered and, having dropped out again, began working at Renco, a manufacturer of optical equipment. He began to drink, concealing it from Gale.

After his domestic relationship with Gale ended, he thought of returning to Utah to finish his degree, but instead enrolled at Berkeley. There followed a ragged record of disenrollment and reinstatement, and more alcohol ("I am becoming so disgusted with myself and my projected future, that I almost, no, I really do dread discovering myself even to you"),[53] but he managed to graduate in 1978.

He earned a teaching credential from San Francisco State but couldn't land a full-time job and began substitute teaching. In 1982 he turned down a full-time position at a middle school in South San Francisco because he was working on his master's degree: "My father would croak if he knew it, but I was offered a job teaching English at the South City's best middle school, and I turned it down feeling that this is my one chance to try for a degree." In the first semester Joel dropped two of his three courses because he found them "intolerable." He took an incomplete in the remaining course because he couldn't write the required paper on Dickens. By February, in what would have been his second semester, he decided not to pursue the master's. He never completed the degree, and there followed a dozen more years of a meager living earned by substituting and home teaching, years punctuated by short-lived and unfulfilled plans to gain a more lucrative and stable position, for example, through earning a math credential.

[52] Gale, e-mail to me, October 30, 2002.
[53] Letter, April 26, 1976.

Hole. Vacant interiority.

Home teaching (1). "If I tell you I've been doing nothing to speak of, I'm not lying. So, I shouldn't have anything to say, right? Fine, I don't! I take a shower, sometimes I shave, sometimes I don't; I have breakfast (nothing worth mentioning); then I putz about until my students call to cancel their home teaching appointments and I have lunch (nothing too much, you understand); I watch a little t.v.; have supper . . . dinner . . . call it what you may, it's no big deal; then I go to bed and sleep. . . . What I'm telling you is that a thing like this is like what my teachers taught me about what a finger is: nothing to count on. Home teaching is, therefore, precisely the job for me. It is a job which, on many levels, one does not do. One is a teacher even when one does not see the student; one teaches the student, but nothing is learned, thus one teaches nothing; and for the many nothings one does, one earns a just wage."[54]

[54] Letter, April 19, 1995.

Home teaching (2). "Being human beings (rather than class members), tutorial students tend to be main characters of engrossing stories. One student, an award-winning baseball-playing honors student, was suddenly stricken by what doctors finally, during the third week of his hospitalization, said was a virus, resulting in the paralysis of one arm and both legs; another was a 15-year-old wisp of a girl suffering since infancy from rheumatoid arthritis, the effects of which include recurrent fevers and painful and debilitating destruction of joints requiring repeated meliorative surgery, in her case mostly in the hands; and another, also 15, was a charmingly demure, generous-hearted Philippine girl dying of leukemia, who returned with her mother to Manila for a final Christmas at her family home."[55]

[55] Letter, January 25, 1987.

Impasse. I want to know why Joel chose November as the month to die. The seventeenth. Friday. Was there any significance to the date? Some circle traversed? I ask Richard when Joel was born, thinking there might be a relationship between the anniversary of his birth and the day he chose to die.

"May," he says. "Do you need the exact date?"

It might be helpful; it might not. I do not know what will help, if anything. I'm looking for some way to puzzle out why November, some sequence. I ask: "Do you remember when Joel's mother died?"

He shakes his head no, gets up from his chair at the computer where he is working and says, "I'm going to take a shower." It is two o'clock in the afternoon.

As he goes upstairs I ask, "What factors do you think fed into the date he chose to kill himself?"

From the top step, not looking down at me, Richard says: "I think he killed himself when he had settled his affairs."

Informed consumer. How did he educate himself? Did he frequent gun shops, check out weapons books from the public library? There are books detailing methods of committing suicide, in the how-to, self-help mode, as well as gun catalogs and gun shows. Did he consult anyone for advice? Read magazines? Was the process slow until he narrowed the field to his weapon of choice? Can you try a gun out and return it?

Inheritance. "The soundest way of acquiring a collection," saith Walter Benjamin. "For a collector's attitude toward his possessions stems from an owner's feeling of responsibility toward his property. Thus it is, in the highest sense, the attitude of an heir, and the most distinguished trait of a collection will always be its transmissibility."[56]

Benjamin makes me feel a bit guilty about the animus with which I've portrayed Joel's conveyance of his things. An heir of the better sort has a duty of care toward items that have been infused with a feeling of responsibility,[57] about which, in Joel's case, there can be no doubt. No matter how paltry the item, he was invested in its transferal into our hands. Though he threw things out, he didn't just throw them,[58] no matter how worthless they might have been in a monetary sense. One does not get rid of a thing lightly, he believed; rather, one exerts oneself to find a home for it, like a lost dog, and a continuing use.

[56] Walter Benjamin, "Unpacking My Library," in *Illuminations*, ed. Hannah Arendt, trans. Harry Zohn (New York: Schocken, 1986), 66.

[57] Of course an heir of the better sort gets the inheritance in the normal sequence: a death occurs and then the inheritance. We received our bounty before Joel died, a reversal entailed by the difficulty of getting the items to us.

[58] A stark contrast to my own sense of things. There are 132 files in my My Documents folder that contain the word *trash*. If Joel were here, he'd want to protest, *How come you have these 132 files if you are not a collector?*

Yet he did not show the same concern for the meaning behind the object, did not tell the story that would have explained its worth (the son's silent echo of the unforthcoming father in **Spin the bottle**). I was made heir to an assemblage of things whose stories I did not know. It was for me to accept at face value—on the evidence of his bothering to convey the object, his silent testimony—this truth: the object was valuable, a presumption helped along by the objects' utility (see **World's Fair**). His investment of feeling, accompanied by deflection of questions about why he cared that we have his computer, books, and microscope, may explain Joel's frustration with Richard's slowness to follow his instructions (see **Mouse**).

Benjamin also insists on the human frailty of collecting: "The phenomenon of collecting loses its meaning as it loses its personal owner."[59] Does this remark indicate that Joel's items minus Joel have been emptied of meaning? Hardly so. It indicates instead that only my ownership preserves meaning, and that this meaning is my responsibility. However, the meaning of objects cannot be preserved, despite their transmissibility, for they take on a new charge with a new owner. The objects had a meaning peculiar to Joel, which we were uninformed about. When his collection was transferred to us, inherited, it was changed. It became the collection of a suicide, and that is the only meaning it can have for me as heir.

Heir to what exactly? What am I heir to, what am I to remember, to safekeep? I experience a double consciousness and double vision: the objects' meaning to Joel in his life, the objects alive, as it were, because Joel housed them in his life; and the meaning to me postsuicide, with Joel no longer living through his objects, but interred within.

[59] Benjamin, "Unpacking My Library," 63.

In remembrance. The decision to die was secret. We did not know how to interpret the changes in Joel that we observed. Richard and I saw surface differences but did not properly attach the changes to their cause. Joel derived pleasure in keeping his secret, sheltering it, pleased to see that no one knew what alone he knew. Perverse though it may seem, Joel assumed a larger degree of control in deciding his affairs in death than he did in life. Death did not overtake him or surprise him. He authored its ending.

It is not the ending I would have written. I choose to remember Joel. Even though he did his best to die in an empty corner, to write over his life with suicide, I refuse to erase his name from love's ledger.

Intimates. Few. Who is there to speak of him? Knock, knock. Me.

Invisible ink. There are those who have kept a journal since they were sixteen. Every letter written or received is organized and meticulously maintained. And there are those who don't. When the collector dies, survivors are overwhelmed by the documentation. When Joel died, we were left with a record of erasure. In an age driven by people who want to be known, Joel disagreed. If one could write a life in invisible ink, he would have.

Kidney failure. In the aftermath, survivors look for a reason, a cause, a correlation. Richard culled passages from Joel's letters from the last months, piecing together the decision to die. He put a chronology together (see **Timeline**), supplied linkages between events, and found a rationalizing framework. In Richard's view, Joel's decision could be well explained. He had no one to love him and live with him, to ease his difficulties. He suffered from neuropathy and the side effects of medications to control its pain and from ongoing anxiety about finances. Take away any of these factors—make him an ordinarily employed man with a reliable job that paid him enough for modest comfort, or halt the creeping deterioration of the nervous system—and he would likely have continued on.

But dangle before him the hope of escape from his dilemma, then take hope away, and the result was fatal. In the spring his affluent father, at age eighty, was hospitalized for a diabetes-related health crisis. It was doubtful that he would survive; his kidneys were "expected to fail." Joel agitated with his brother about getting their father's financial affairs in order and was aware of his unseemly hopes: "I'm not ready to go into the exhaustive explanation of my thoughts and feelings regarding my father that I think it would take to make my ungenerous fears concerning the coming summer (not to speak of the coming years) seem less blamable. So I'll leave my father's and my future for another letter."[60] He talked hopefully of moving out to the East Bay near Barbara, of a little house, of getting a dog and a goat.

But his father survived, and Joel did not escape by means of an inheritance. Father and son were on a seesaw. Someone had to die, and his father lived.

[60] Letter, April 19, 1995.

The knocking at the gate in *Macbeth*. In February 1976, eight months after his mother's death, Joel undertook a critical analysis of *Macbeth* in an essay for **English 1B**. He was a good student, intelligent, engaged, and comfortable with the sometimes arcane and peculiar terms in which academic critics discuss literature. Despite their peculiarity—maybe *because* of their peculiarity—in these terms he could respond to the loss of his mother, writing about her without openly writing about her.

Joel's point of attack in the essay is Macbeth's state of mind when he delivers his soliloquy in act 5, addressed to the black vast after he learns that Lady Macbeth is dead:

> She should have died hereafter;
> There would have been a time for such a word.
> To-morrow, and to-morrow, and to-morrow,
> Creeps in this petty pace from day to day
> To the last syllable of recorded time,
> And all our yesterdays have lighted fools
> The way to dusty death. Out, out, brief candle!
> Life's but a walking shadow, a poor player
> That struts and frets his hour upon the stage
> And then is heard no more: it is a tale
> Told by an idiot, full of sound and fury,
> Signifying nothing.

Macbeth's words emerge from a split in the world, according to Joel, a division between our normal moral order and the one in which Macbeth overcomes his scruples and murders King Duncan to seize the throne. Joel develops this thought by means of a detour through Thomas De Quincey.

> De Quincey . . . wrote an essay, "The Knocking at the Gate in *Macbeth*," in which he discusses the significance of the knocking at the gate, following the murder of Duncan, as awakening us to the fact that the murder has occurred in a state of detachment—in a world of its own: the knocking brings us back into the world of nature, good, and all that stuff. It is a situation of intense opposition to the moral order and it is seen to be one in which the characters, falling out of Grace, are alienated from the world. They have no control over the ultimate results of their actions, their words speak greater truths than the meanings they'd intended, it goes on and on.[61]

A state of detachment. A world of its own. Where in this is Joel's mother? Where is Joel? Let me remember: the words of people in a counterworld like Macbeth's *speak greater truths than the meanings they'd intended*.

[61] Letter, February 1976.
Joel describes the essay
in his letter.

Lady Macbeth. Joel's essay asked a version of the question I have asked (see **chain, chain, chain**): How did Macbeth assess, how did he feel about his wife's death? I want to draw from his answer an insight into Joel's feelings about his mother, and through them to answer the questions Joel's actions posed to me. I know that I will not discover an answer, of course. I will only make myself another link on the chain of interpretation.

Me : Joel : Mother :: Joel : Macbeth : Lady Macbeth.

Joel's discussion of the play begins with Macbeth's soliloquy:

I call your attention to "Macbeth" V.v.17: "She should have died hereafter. . . ." What do you notice about it? What you notice about it is that there is no clear referent. "It" should be carefully tied to a noun or noun phrase. But, ignoring my grammar for the moment, what is notable about the opening of this soliloquy? It is ambiguous! Yes! Every critic who has discussed the soliloquy has mentioned that the line is ambiguous as if the word, "ambiguous," were terrifying and the task of resolving the ambiguity an heroic deed. One writer is so awe-struck with the ambiguity of the line that he insists that Macbeth means all the standard interpretations at once and is "groping for meanings."[62] The standard meanings are: 1) She would have died eventually anyhow; 2) It would have been better for her to have died some day in the future when things would have been more peaceful, etc. The diction is too grand, too compatible with the armchair mood in which the play is normally experienced, to allow Macbeth to have meant anything so mean, so despicable as what the line seems to say: "Stupid wench—she should have died hereafter: there's a time for everything and this was certainly not the time for her to go and croak."[63]

Joel's word "armchair" is intriguing: he uses it to reject a critical attitude identified by one meaning of the word (unengaged, remote, theoretical) while he sits in the same chair (vicariously living through another's experiences). He will think about his mother's suicide, that is, in the guise of Lady Macbeth's.

Joel rejects the critical resort to ambiguity by the armchair critics and passionately engages Macbeth's barbarous remarks, taking the lines to mean what they seem to mean, that Macbeth believes he is a fit judge of the right time for someone else to die:

The fact is . . . that Macbeth had become, by that time, enough of a tyrant, sufficiently over-confident and egomaniacal to have thought himself an adequate judge of when people should live and die. It didn't suit him for his wife to die at that moment. Why? God only knows—the guy was a loony, you know. Anyhow, that's what he meant when he said it. But by the time he's progressed to the final word of the second line ("There would have been a time for such a *word*") he is no longer

[62] Joel is quoting L. C. Knights, *Some Shakespearean Themes: And an Approach to "Hamlet"* (Stanford: Stanford University Press, 1959), 131.
[63] Letter, February 1976.

talking simply about the death of his wife: He's moved on to a level of abstraction in which lives and deaths are only syllables and words making up the "tale told by an idiot."

Here again is the division in Macbeth's world, with a level of living and a level of abstraction from it. Can I imagine the same sort of division in Joel? Despite the differences between the life circumstances of the undergraduate literature student and those of the king of Scotland, Joel draws himself into parallel with Macbeth. His emotional state was a version of Macbeth's. He, too, confronted a death, that of his mother. Like the "loony" Macbeth, he was "bonkers," for he was suffering at the time of this analysis from penetrating memories of the very sort that later led him (in **Time travel**) to that self-description. And at the end of his discussion of the play, he describes his ego as "boundless," implicitly comparing himself to the "ego-maniacal" nobleman.

For both Macbeth and Joel time is compressed, and death is not the distant thing it might be for most men. Macbeth can only wish it tarried a while, not see it as distant. That is why he doesn't respond to Lady Macbeth's death with "She shouldn't have died, period." For this compression in Joel, see **Onset**.

Suppose, then, that we listen to the soliloquy as Joel/Macbeth speaks his bitter lines: "Stupid wench—she should have died hereafter: there's a time for everything and this was certainly not the time for her to go and croak."

Larry. A majestic golden retriever. "It must be a great comfort," said Joel, "to have him lying at your feet." If I ask what gift might have kept Joel alive, I think: a companion.

On the Beara Peninsula in western Ireland an old sheepdog kept watch from the driveway and hill above our B&B. I tried to befriend him, but he'd have nothing of it. He didn't even turn his head in my direction when I spoke.

The proprietress said, "Oh, he only has eyes for his master. In all the many years we've had him, he's only looked at me twice, really looked at me." The master was her husband, who had rescued the dog from a sheep keeper. The young dog was overzealous and anxious to please and would herd the flock toward the edge of a cliff. In anger his owner had beaten the feckless animal. The master had intervened and taken him for his own, and the old sheepdog had never forgotten. In our days at the B&B, he waited for his master's return with unbroken concentration.

When the man returned from work at the end of the day and trudged the steep road, what did he see as his coming was eyed in the dusky air? He saw this world healed and whole, where love inhuman, boundless, moves and barks at petty cares.

I would give Joel this gift:

See him standing on the hills above the brilliant waters east of the bay, ears pricked to catch a thrumming in the wind, eyes alert for a sudden—to me invisible—movement in the grass, nose moist like a bitten plum, nostrils flexing in and out. He sees me raise my eyes to him, turns his muscled shoulders toward the decline of the sloping hill, and runs without caution, with abandon, wildly, joyfully, past picnic table, house, and garage, past everything, to me.[64]

[64] Adapted from Marcia Aldrich, "The Dead Dog Essay," *Florida Review* 34, no. 1 (2009): 79–88.

To Joel, on no
occasion
12 July 1989
"now again / My
thoughts are
children"

To Richard &
Marcia, on the
occasion of my
return to your
home I'd never
visited and
thus had never
left...
1 October 1995

Last visit. The installation of his haunting. In October he drove across the country in his Ford Escort wagon with bad tires, having stuffed it with belongings he wanted us to have (see **Arborvitae**). When he arrived, the flowers were so deep in color that they had the power to heal. A week's imitation of a life—a life shared in our life.

He held all the cards. He knew he was saying good-bye for all time, and we did not. He savored to a fare-thee-well every last *last*: the last concert, the last conversation, the last dinner.

The morning of his departure, I was in the shower. He never said good-bye. Backing out of the driveway, steering to the left, and pulling away—that's the film that runs in my head.

Among the books Joel delivered on his last visit were the Jerusalem Bible, a concordance to Shakespeare, Oxford companions to English and American literature and the theater, an Oxford classical dictionary, and Philip Larkin's *Collected Poems*, regifted, which he inscribed, "To Richard & Marcia, on the occasion of my return to your home I'd never visited and thus had never left. . . ."

Last words to me. A cheerful list of objects. When almost nothing was left in his apartment, he sent the remainder to me. On Friday afternoon, November 17, a package arrived at our door. Inside were a small box and a short letter, addressed to me and dated two days earlier.

15 November

Dear Marcia,

According to television advertising, 'tis the season, so Merry Christmas!

In case the contents aren't self-explanatory, here's a brief inventory:

- a partial roll of old pennies & one or two Canadian coins...

- one of the final run of $2 bills, and a silver dollar of I-don't-remember-what significance...

- a couple of Chicago World's Fair commemoration spoons

- an egg coddler with a surprise inside

- my favorite reading supporter button

Love,
Joel

Dear Marcia,

According to television advertising, 'tis the season, so Merry Christmas!

In case the contents aren't self-explanatory, here's a brief inventory:

- a partial roll of old pennies & one or two Canadian coins . . .
- one of the final run of $2 bills, and a silver dollar of I-don't-remember-what significance
- a couple of Chicago World's Fair commemorative spoons
- an **egg coddler** with a surprise inside
- my favorite reading supporter button.

Love,

Joel

The surprise was one thousand dollars in cash, presumably from the sale of his car.

The note was just enough to convey the items and let me know from whom they came. I can't explain why he needed to itemize the contents and pen a few comments. I have no idea why he referred to a Christmas he wouldn't be alive to see. Perhaps he really felt cheery.

Last words to Richard. His letters, once full of frustration, financial worries, his unsteady cars, anxiety, and poor health, became blankly anonymous. "Are you entirely, perfectly happy? Or do you find yourself unhappy in response to bills, complaining children, or the failure of American schools to acquaint students with the novels of early Soviet socialists?[65] Or worse, are you sometimes being unhappy about things that ought to be making you a happier, more contented person?"[66] These last words to Richard were written as if addressed to an anonymous recipient in the style of the absurd. He made no mention of his recent visit to us. He spoke from beyond the reach of unhappiness, from a calm spot out of the fray wherein struggle those of us who are not posthumous.

[65] Joel was amused by his own fondness for Gladkov's much-maligned Soviet realist novel *Cement*.

[66] Letter, October 22, 1995.

Literary criticism. The more diffident Joel became, the more I wanted to understand him. He became a great, difficult poem that unsettles and exhausts me and that I never get to the end of understanding.

Macbeth. Less than a year after his mother's death and two decades before his own, Joel asked: If life is meaningless, why doesn't Macbeth kill himself? Let me play therapist for the moment and respond to this question with another: If life is meaningless, why doesn't Joel kill himself in 1976?

What keeps Macbeth going, according to Joel's analysis, is the separation between two orders, a "division in Macbeth's world, with a level of living and a level of abstraction from it" (see **Lady Macbeth**)—the natural world and an alienated world-of-its-own. Macbeth is able to continue on because life, though meaningless, is an abstraction from which he is separate, doing his living in the other realm.

> Now, one of the wonders of my analysis is that it allows for some explanation of why, if life is so meaningless, does Macbeth not kill himself. It is because Life, an abstract thing, not something to do with living, is meaningless and onerous; but Macbeth is something quite apart from that, in opposition to it, in fact. He believes he bears a "charmed life"—he has nothing to do with time or death.[67]

[67] Letter, February 1976.

Such is Macbeth's (that is, Macbeth/Joel's) answer to the philo-sophical question:[68] Does the absurdity of life require suicide?

Should I say, then, that Joel suffered from the same derange-ment as Macbeth, putting the meaningless suffering of his mother, all the world's meaningless suffering, on the other side of a wall that divided sorrow from the realm in which he did his living? Perhaps his mother and Joel, from this time on, occupied different orders, and that is what kept him going. In favor of that notion is Joel's two-decade-long silence about his mother after his essay about her in English IA.

But there is another view: that Joel, an unpartitioned human being, and a more consistent thinker than the rant-ing Macbeth, built no wall, and lived on the side of suffering, where there was no reason he should not kill himself. It just took a long time to do.

Still I say, no matter how long it took, he should have died hereafter.

[68] The only philosophical question, accord-ing to Albert Camus, *The Myth of Sisyphus and Other Essays*, trans. Justin O'Brien (New York: Knopf, 1955).

Manhattan (list of lists of reasons that life is worth living).

In the movie by Woody Allen, his alter ego comes up with the following:

Groucho Marx
Willie Mays
the second movement of Mozart's Jupiter Symphony
Louis Armstrong's "Potato Head Blues"
Swedish movies
Flaubert's *A Sentimental Education*
Marlon Brando
Frank Sinatra
apples and pears by Cézanne
crabs at Sam Wo's
Tracy's face (guised in the movie by Mariel Hemingway)

This assortment of favorites is absorbed and digested, by implication, in Gale's **toast**.

 Such fondnesses have little to do with refusing suicide, which a person chooses because his calendar of tomorrows is full of suffering. It is not the nearness of the end but interminable time that takes away a person's tastes. Otherwise there would be no last meal for the condemned convict, no cancered man relishing an artichoke, no last visit. It is the absence of choice that allows the condemned to taste his last meal.

The ability to assemble a roster of tastes probably does, however, imply that one is not suicidal.

To suppose a list for Joel (who never liked Woody Allen), one less earnest than *Manhattan's* and pulled from different moments of his life:

Bach's English Suites
Dietrich Fischer-Dieskau
Pete's Wicked Ale
The Hitchhiker's Guide to the Galaxy
Rhodesian ridgebacks
Claes Oldenburg's deflated sculptures
Frisbee
Julie Newmar
David Copperfield
Sonny Terry and Brownie McGhee
Soupy Sales

At the final stage:

~~Bach's English Suites~~
~~Dietrich Fischer-Dieskau~~
~~Pete's Wicked Ale~~
~~*The Hitchhiker's Guide to the Galaxy*~~
~~Rhodesian ridgebacks~~
~~Claes Oldenburg's deflated sculptures~~
~~Frisbee~~
~~Julie Newmar~~
~~*David Copperfield*~~
~~Sonny Terry and Brownie McGhee~~
~~Soupy Sales~~

Marital status. Never married.

Men on women: cinema verité. During the period he lived with Joel, Richard kept a journal, from which Joel is strikingly absent. It does, however, re-create one conversation between them, built on the male principle of chasing women,[69] or better, the tingle of talking about chasing women:

> Now it is Sunday night. Joel tells me that he's had a drink of vodka and it hasn't done anything to him. I consider a reply. I seem to spend so much time considering replies. They must be witty, dry, and lead the conversation on if possible—maybe have a question implied. I might say to him, "You've got plenty more to get the job done." But that doesn't seem right.
>
> "It's going to be a long night," he says. He is starting springy little steps and shadowboxing.
>
> "Why don't you go for a long walk?"
>
> "I would but I'm afraid to because of the rain."
>
> I rinse out my cereal bowl. "Would you melt like the Wicked Witch of the West?"
>
> "I'm concerned about aggravating my cold in the damp."

[69] See **The underlying, unifying principle of a life**.

I don't believe you get colds from the rain but I decide not to say so. I have an unclear memory of having that argument with him before.

"I've got all this nervous energy. I think I'm wound up because of Karen." He does this. He drops her name into the conversation as if I know who Karen is.

"Who's Karen?"

"She's the one from work I'm going to see *Taxi Driver* with tomorrow night."[70] He had mentioned earlier in the evening that he was going to see *Taxi Driver*. Maybe he really believes he mentioned Karen then. I had put up calendars from some of the rerun movie houses and he made a joke about how it was nice of me to do that so we could relive our youth.

"How old is Karen?" I inquire. He had mentioned a girl at work before—she is twenty-two or so.

"Twenty-one. I really don't want to get involved with her. First of all, she's not that attractive. You know how you get involved with these women and in maybe a year you step back and say, yech, how did I ever do that." The alcohol is working now. Earlier in the evening he had wanted to mention the date; now he feels free enough.

"Yes, one wants to be proud of one's ex's," I say.

"I don't want anything to happen with her—I mean I don't want anything to happen, if you know what I mean."

"You mean it's a hands-off affair. Well I'm sure you'll be perfectly composed."

"I hope so." He throws some punches. "It's her I'm concerned about."

"Well I'm sure you're the most sophisticated and intelligent thing to come into her young life so far." I go into the bathroom to brush my teeth. He follows into the hall.

[70] See **Salesman**.

"Yeah, I catch the sarcasm. But in reality one often discovers when one enters the work world after some years in the University that one is more sophisticated than one's fellow workers."

"Well I've found that true wherever I go," I say cleverly.

"It certainly wasn't true for me, not at Berkeley. All those graduate students, you know."

"That doesn't bother me because I'm a graduate student," I again riposte. I start to floss my teeth.

"The one I really wish I had held onto was Roxana."

I start when I hear her name. Now I'm interested. "It doesn't seem to me as I recall that you went after her very hard."

"Well it soon became clear what kind of relationship she wanted."

"You mean a father."

"I don't know. Anyway she was in love with this body over at the swimming pool where she lifeguarded." He has his hands locked on the upper doorway and is rocking to and fro in the door.

"I don't trust women who fall in love with bodies." I throw my floss into the wastebasket and think about what I mean by this.

"Actually, you didn't find her as attractive as I did, as I recall." This surprises the hell out of me. I found her very attractive. In fact, what I remember most about the whole affair is how he made damn sure she and I never made connections again after I met her at his house.[71] After that meeting I suggested to him that we all go see *King Kong* together. He never got around to mentioning it to

[71] Richard is recalling an earlier incident, before he and Joel were living together.

her. Then once when I came over he announced she had called while I was in transit and invited us to a party that night—but he didn't feel like drinking, it would be too late, etc. It's part of the case I make when I accuse him of jealousy.

But I say, "No, I thought she was good-looking but not as much as you did."

"Of course, I thought she was some kind of bronze goddess." We laugh. "I thought maybe you liked that other one better, what's her name . . ." This is another routine. He can't remember anyone's name. I have to remind him of what his friends' names are. I decide not to this time. I know who he's talking about.

"No, I didn't," I reply. "She was too neurotic for me."

"That's for sure. She's the only one who broke the rule I had. I wouldn't let a woman sleep at my place unless she slept with me. But she stayed over one night."

I take my contact lenses out and come out of the bathroom. "You know the only reason you liked Roxana so much is that she was so big. You've got this thing about tall women."

"That's not the only reason—but I like tall women."

"I should introduce you to Rhonda. She's a big girl."

"What good would that do me? I could admire her physique and make figure studies or something."

"Listen, you can't do any worse than I'm doing. I'm not getting anything out of her." We go into the living room.

"I remember when I decided to make the grand experiment with Roxana, so to speak. I went over to her place and brought my toothbrush. I knew it wasn't going to happen. But I decided, in the interests of the questioning intellect"—he shoves his fist forward in mock emphasis—"to give it a try. So in about an hour I said, 'Enough studying. It's time for bed.' I left soon after that."[72]

There's much I might say about this conversation and its precise cruelties, but I'll limit myself to this: I was never privy to talk between Joel and Richard of such duration.

[72] Richard's journal, January 7, 1979. With retrospective chagrin he says of this material, "It reveals that I had rudiments of self-knowledge, and that a little self-knowledge is a dangerous thing."

Mentor. Joel and I had a conversation over dinner, Richard having been called away by a phone call. We sat across from one another at the table, candles burning between us. Suddenly Joel said, "I can't tell you what pleasure I have in seeing Richard exceed my expectations." He was speaking in his old role of mentor, a teacher who feels satisfaction in his best student's achievements. He was looking at Richard with the eyes of the soon-to-be-departed. He was looking at him for what he alone knew would be the last time, gauging how far Richard had come from the boy kicking down the hot streets of Reseda.

I realize that much now, but then I felt his remark as a rebuke, as if I didn't sufficiently appreciate my own husband. Around Richard and Joel I sometimes stepped into the pages of a D. H. Lawrence novel, say *Women in Love*, and was cast against my will as the irritating and cloying Ursula. When we three were together, I felt a tagalong on their outings. A possessiveness came over me, and I felt jealous of the attention Richard paid Joel, as he was jealous of me.

Method. Long summers ago I picked up my son at a friend's house and noticed black smoke pouring from the second-story windows of the house down the street. A middle-aged woman, living only with her cat after a divorce, had doused her bed with kerosene and set herself alight. The firefighters rescued the cat, but it was too late to save the woman, whom they found in the bathtub. The firefighters speculated that she was trying to put out the fire, which was herself. She may have had second thoughts, or was unprepared for the pain. See **Gun**.

Money. Joel's father asked Richard, "Was it money? I offered him money." Yes, it was money, thought Richard, but he did not want it to be *offered*. See **Kidney failure** and **Thanksgiving**.

More forest. "I think we ought to read only the kind of books that wound and stab us. If the book we're reading doesn't wake us up with a blow on the head, what are we reading it for? . . . But we need the books that affect us like a disaster, that grieve us deeply, like the death of someone we loved more than ourselves, like a being banished into forests far from everyone, like a suicide."[73]

[73] Franz Kafka to Oskar Pollak, January 27, 1904, in *Letters to Friends, Family, and Editors*, trans. Richard and Clara Winston (New York: Schocken, 1977), 16.

Mother's Day. "The holidays have since elementary school days
   meant appreciation of the suffering my presence in the world
   brought those to whom I owe more than my puny powers
   and monstrous incapacities would ever allow me to produce
   in compensation. My holiday craft projects prepared amidst
   the construction paper, glue and confusion that along with
   baseball and square dancing made school hateful to me were
   concretions of ineptitude. Giving them was like having a severe
   stutter and being forced to say I am s-orry I s-s-tutututer."[74]

[74] Joel, Mother's Day card
   to me, May 10, 1987.

Mouse. Joel's bequeathed computer was Richard's introduction to use of this interface. He was clumsy at first, and Joel was impatient and irritated in his instruction on how to use it. It was in this irritation that the supreme effort Joel's performance required broke through his mask.

Neuropathy, diabetic. Degeneration of the nervous system
caused by high blood glucose and other factors. In January
1994, Joel began to suffer pain in his right leg; it was so severe
by late February that getting into, driving, and getting out of
his car was nearly impossible. Fearing loss of his livelihood,
he saw a neurologist. The diagnosis was neuropathy, "meaning
my nervous system is degenerating in what, in the absence of
Greek, they would be forced to describe as being in an aging
diabetic kind of way."[75] He took medication to control the pain,
but it had side effects, weakening his memory and constricting
his ability to speak. Common words began to slip away from
him, the names of simple things.

[75] Letter, March 19, 1994.

Note. I wanted Joel to leave a note behind that bore the traces of his disaster, to bear the traces of his having reduced himself to a ghostlike status, a disappearing man. (Perhaps the eradicating of the personal is that trace.)

Now he tells us. "History decays into images, not into stories."[76]

[76] Walter Benjamin, *The Arcades Project*, trans. Howard Eiland and Kevin McLaughlin (Cambridge: Belknap Press of Harvard University Press, 1999), 476.

Oban. Reluctant to depart, he stayed longer than we expected. On Joel's last full day, Richard accompanied him to the Goodyear store, where he bought a replacement for a worn tire to which the long journey back across plains and mountains would certainly prove fatal. We ate dinner, and Richard attended a meeting of the school parent council, while I worked on my classes, and last we assembled for a benediction and farewell with a single malt from the intricate coast of western Scotland, Oban.

We sat at the white-tile table in the small, unremodeled, and rather hard kitchen, built at the end of the Depression, with its gray eggshell walls, white trim, and single burgundy-purple Formica countertop. Richard took his spot at one end of the table, I mine at the other, while Joel sat between, facing the wall on which hung a big reproduction of Hopper's *Tables for Ladies*. There was not much drinking, just a glass each of Oban, nor much talk, but desultory breaks in the silence, splashes on the seashore, light wrack and spray cast up from an ocean of words that none of us could say.

Swirl the gold in my glass, lift the liquid to my lips, and taste: seaside brine and mist on my palate. In the nose, smoke and something vanishing, not the scotch but borne by it, textureless: the forgettable in that night, all that which I have forgotten. And underneath, mouth-filling, in the long finish . . . *myself*.

I had first met Joel thirteen years earlier when, in the spring of 1982, he had flown to Seattle for a visit. Richard and I were still in graduate school, living in a one-bedroom apartment, and Joel slept on our couch. He had seen women come and go, and I was still a relative newcomer. He had watched Richard grow up, transform himself from adolescent to young man, on the cusp of becoming a professional. He was a scholar of Richard's history, while I was still learning the alphabet.

One afternoon we three went bowling, my second or third lifetime stab at the game, and though neither of them had bowled in years, they fell into competition with one another. Richard rolled the highest score, Joel not far behind, while I was the also-ran, too often in the gutter to figure in the competition. I could only be the object of instruction, spurred by an anxiousness that I show myself worthy: *Don't swing your arm so wide, don't begin your approach from so far back, don't* . . . I was at once between and outside them.

Now Richard's life was, through me, more established than Joel's, yet on this last night, drinks in hand, the prior bond between them was still palpable. It was they who loved solitude, stoicism, and silence, and I tasted, in my glass, the awkward intruder.

One more thing in the glass, too, in the last sip, underneath and farther back on the tongue than the rest, or maybe I should call it the mouth that shapes all, the rocky shore that breaks the waves. It was my old story, exclusion from two people who shared a prior bond: my sisters—my half sisters—ten and twelve years older than I, born to my mother when she was a different wife.[77]

Swirling the gold in his glass, what did Richard taste? A sense of disappointment, the Oban lighter than his favorites, Talisker and Lagavulin, those peaty bog monsters. He had gone to the

[77] See Marcia Aldrich, "Balance," in *Girl Rearing*.

Shop-Rite armed with the rare occasion to splurge on a single malt, and he wanted to try something new—like his mother, who, with a hundred family-pleasing recipes in her rotation, periodically put on the table a new dish, which the family usually consumed in silence, as if filling out an application, and which she pronounced "interesting," her lowest rating. In Richard the impulse to try the new is allied with an occasional carelessness, putting a book on the syllabus he hasn't read, letting the dog off leash in the field when I would not, minor things, and then with something not minor—indifference, resignation, perhaps. If the Oban was quiet, it was for him the silence of this last night, the summing up and the well-wishes never spoken. He felt that he had chosen the wrong scotch.

In Joel's glass, control. He did not want to drink too much. He did not want the alcohol to loosen him. He did not want to say too much, for what could he say? He sat, arms straight, holding the glass in studied silence. I do not know where he went between sips. Did he stay with us on this last evening, savoring the finish, the denouement? It may have been so. Or perhaps he visited his father, or his mother. Or looked ahead, to the dread trip home, the reality of his last weeks, this night the final taste of anyone who loved him.

Onset. Joel believed always that he would live a shortened time, and he was a prescient actuary. He told Gale before he was twenty-five that he would not live to fifty.[78] This number was not arbitrary, but the result of a good calculation. The diabetic's life expectancy is at diagnosis one-third less than that of non-diabetics. Pick a rough, common life expectancy at the time of Joel's estimate, say seventy-five, take off one-third, and the result is the limit he named to Gale. But his intuitive calculations were perhaps more precise than that. At thirty-five he described himself as "balanced now upon the midpoint of my three score and ten." Do not take the biblical allotment at face value, but reduce it by the diabetic one-third, and the result is forty-six years and eight months, which predicts, almost to the month, his **age at death.**

"I am going to die," Joel said. "If it will be more convenient, please don't hesitate to grieve 'a little early.'"[79] See **Augury.**

[78] Gale to Richard, August 30, 1996.
[79] Letter, June 9, 1990.

Other women who passed through that I know of. Fran, Becky, Janice, Beth. Some of them mattered for a while. The breakup with Beth prompted an identity crisis (see **Time travel**), and at the end of an evening with Becky, Joel "walked her home, said 'good-night,' and felt the coffin lid closing on me."[80]

[80] Letter, July 31, 1976.

Path (1). A direction constrained by a past direction. The autopsy report described the gunshot wound thusly: "directed left to right, front to back, and downwards, forming angles of two degrees with the horizontal plane. Through the skin and muscles of the scalp, then penetrates the skull and travels through the cortex of the brain, including the basal ganglia and ventricles, and terminates through the skull and beneath the scalp on the right posterior parietal region."

Path (2). I was driving my daughter to a football game at the high school and I ran into a young boy.

I had turned the corner onto the street fronting the school where cars were pulling to the side of the road to let their kids out. From out of nowhere a boy ran right in front of me, or at least at the time he seemed to come from nowhere. It was as if he fell out of the sky. Driving slowly, even so I couldn't brake fast enough or swerve out of his path. I heard a thud and then he bounced to the side of the road. He lay on the curb for just a second, a second in which I thought my heart would explode, and then he sprang up, coming back to life. I pulled to the side jaggedly, sticking half out into the road, my car door open, stumbled out and ran to him. At the same time his father was running to his son. When I reached him, his father already had his arms around him, and said, "He's all right. A little shaken up, but fine." I started to cry. The boy said it was his fault; he had run in front of me; there was nothing I could do.

My daughter proceeded to her game, and I drove to a nearby park and slumped over the steering wheel, crying. Whether it was my fault or his fault, I hit a boy. What did it matter, finally, if it was his fault or mine. Assigning blame did nothing when the result could have been his body lying still in the grass. I was lucky. The collision wasn't fatal, wasn't final, the boy got up and resumed his life. It wasn't an important failure for anyone else, but the illusion that I could never hurt someone, that I don't hurt anyone, was shattered.

Path (3). "Last week was brutally difficult. I got myself locked into a four-day assignment in the classroom of a teacher whose reputation for immaturity and self-indulgence continues to grow well into his thirtieth year in the profession. He relies upon his charm and his promises of uncritical appreciation of his students' 'work' to keep his classroom orderly; he does nothing to establish a more general, abstract sense of decorum, nothing that will remain in his absence. His substitutes have left an unusual trail of bitter resentment and promises never again to be so used. I stuck it out four days and was gnashing my teeth. A substitute must see the same students in a number of classrooms each semester; any loss of credibility due to the failure to discipline in any one classroom results in an almost geometric multiplication of ill-effects and animosity. Victimization is an important part of a substitute's career; you cannot expect, shouldn't hope to be used fairly. It was, as I said, a difficult week, but I survived, as I always seem to, though it may be less certain that I will always seek to."[81]

[81] Letter, November 23, 1984.

Path (4). The snow, soft and heavy, is falling, and the blood is flowing to my heart. As I stop at a red light, I see a boy tearing down Hagadorn and sweeping right onto Burcham. I am alarmed at his speed, the danger he is courting. Where can he be going at this hour, what can he be doing in this weather? Has he no parents, no one to look after him and keep him home on such an evening? Hardly anyone is out this late in the snow, and the few I see are tucked securely in their cars. No one walks a dog or is out for a late run, no one but the boy riding a bike.

The red light turns green, and I creep forward. The snowfall is thick and the wipers can barely sweep the snow aside before the windshield is covered again. I see fragments of the boy ahead, farther ahead of me than I'd ever think possible. Snow sprays behind him. It's beautiful. He jumps his bike over the curb out onto the street, swerves into the middle where the snow is accumulating, accelerates, and turns left onto Butterfield.

This boy on the bike has been outside a long time; that's how he looks to me. My neighbors would say I've made him up. They'd say my ears deceive me when I hear his bike's tires shifting among the shards of ice and the cold wind like one indrawn breath. They see and hear nothing unusual. And for a long time, until Joel died, I didn't either. But now at night with kitchens warm with children and stew, I can't help believe Joel stands at the border of our yards. He carries me beyond the limits of my neighbors. There are always, at every moment, boys falling from the sky.

His bike doesn't seem to touch the road during these maneuvers, it flies left, lands softly, securely, without pause, into the snow, and proceeds. No slipping, sliding, or swerving. I'm closing in on him. I can see his green pants billowing against the white snow, and he's only wearing a vest, a red vest.

He turns onto my street, Orchard.

He's not my son, he's not my husband, he's not Joel. He's just a boy out alone in the snow, and yet I feel a tremendous sense of concern that something might happen to this boy. When he passes my house and continues down the snow-lit street until he's out of view, something is being ripped from me. I haven't known him for long or well. I saw him for the first time a few minutes ago, and yet it feels like an eternity. He has opened a door of feeling.

He's become a regular visitor after everyone has gone to bed. He usually arrives by bike, wheeling it through the back door, its tires packed with snow, into the living room and leaning it against the back of the couch. The handlebars are freezing cold. Sometimes I find him asleep on the couch and I wrap blankets around him and say a silent prayer. His head of dark curls rests on the arm.

Joel's suicide happens in the corner of the picture no one wants to see. If I feel sheltered, there must be someone outside in the snow, exposed. If we are to feel safe and secure in our kitchens and in our beds, there must be someone in the dark, unwrapped.

Pentobarbital. A sedative, a hypnotic, an antispasmodic. Under the trade name Nembutal it killed Marilyn Monroe.

Philosopher. Saving nothing, Joel unharnessed himself from the furniture of his being. Where he was going, he required no baggage. Like Thoreau's philosopher, he stripped his life bare, compacting everything into himself, and could "walk out the gate empty-handed without anxiety."[82] The slightest of shelters was no longer necessary. He savored his plan, executing its parts, checking off each item on a list he might have titled *Last Things*. In his final days he broke his attachment to the last of them and drifted free.

[82] Thoreau, *Walden; or, Life in the Woods*, vol. 1 (Boston: Houghton, Mifflin, 1854), 41. Note also: "I did not wish to live what was not life, living is so dear; nor did I wish to practise resignation, unless it was quite necessary" (143).

Piano four hands. During his visit to Seattle in 1982, we accompanied Joel to a dinner engagement at the home of a woman whose daughter, Laurel, he had been dating. The woman doted on Joel with cuisine and wine, and he became less stiff, more expansive, unreserved. She coaxed him into playing her gleaming grand piano, then joined him in four-handed duets. He was animated and flushed with these measures, recapturing the pleasures of performing as the apple of his mother's eye. It was a night of senses, visual, olfactory, tactile, aural.

On the drive home Joel acknowledged that, of the two women, he felt more fondness for her mother than for Laurel.

Plan. We did not see the subtext beneath Joel's extraordinary behavior, but I ask myself what we would have done if we had. What if we had confronted his impending suicide? If I see that the last fawn is dragging its legs, what am I going to do about it?

Most probably we would have tried to haul Joel back into living, reattaching the broken cords. Maybe he hoped he would be caught when he visited us one last time, dangling binoculars and microscope before us, through which we still could not see. However, confronting Joel's last acts, we confront the limits not only of our knowledge, but of our remedies. If we had probed more deeply, would we have made Joel alter his plans? I think yes, but not in the direction we wanted, steering his course back to the living. He was sailing the black seas, full speed ahead, no turning back. Joel wanted no preventive measures, no intervention. We would have disrupted his **project**, made him carry it out differently than he had planned, which he judged the humane and proper way to die. We would have stolen his gratification and purpose, turned him furtive, like a naughty child or bulimic snacker. We would have burned the script, when the show must go on.

Police. He chose the police—always singular but collective—to discover him because the officers were not friends or relatives but impersonal operatives. Their experience and training would equip them to manage his body, disfigured by a wound. Seeing violence and death is the job of the police. That's why we pay for their patrol, to come across us in our upheaval, twisted and mangled. Joel sheltered any who knew him from such unrest. See **Cassanego.**

Police report. Quoted by the coroner:

> On 11-20-95 at approximately 1600 hours, Officer Cassanego was dispatched to the address on a well-being check. After receiving no response to repeated knocks at the door, he used the key that was sent to the department to enter the secured residence. Once inside, the deceased was found unresponsive. Emergency services were called with Paramedic Vanaart responding. Examination at the scene revealed the deceased to be lying on his left side in the bathroom. He was dressed in street clothes. Noted was an apparent gunshot wound to the left temporal region with no apparent exit. In his left hand was a .38 caliber revolver serial number ADT3201. There was one spent casing under the hammer with the remaining four chambers empty. A box of .38 special ammunition and an empty plastic gun case sat on the counter. The residence was barren. No books, papers, address books, personal clothing were seen.

Prell, Martin. Joel's father, a Lockheed engineer and a diabetic (Joel, then, was at least the third generation). What was he like as father to the son? I did not know him and asked Richard to play proxy:

- IQ of 160 (or was it 170? No, that was Phaedrus in *Zen and the Art of Motorcycle Maintenance*), designer of the control rods, Joel said, in the first nuclear reactor. Could it be true? The **timeline** shows that he was in Chicago in the 1940s when Chicago Pile No. 1 went critical, achieving a self-sustaining fission chain reaction, on page 1 of the history of the second half of the twentieth century.

- Designer of a pair of matching coffee tables in the family living room, glass tops with beveled edge atop a brilliant chromed frame, not austere but simple, powerful, each before a white fabric sofa. He listened with unenthusiasm to Richard's mention of a poured-resin table he'd like to make, a plan picked up loosely from *Popular Science*, roughly woody in the way of the day.

- Designer for commercial production of a strong and steady folding table, he lost the patent, Joel said—with what tone? A hint of filial contempt, a recognition of the financial loss, an appreciation of the energy of the competition, all of these concepts new to Richard's mind at the time.

- A finely perceiving sensor who in 1950, he said, could identify blindfolded the make of a car by the odor of its exhaust.

- Hearer of true sounds, with AR2 loudspeakers, renowned for their refined accuracy, wall-mounted in the living room, wiring unseen, who was brought by Joel to Richard's apartment in Sherman Oaks to hear his speakers, with Heil air motion transformers, which he pronounced too bright, not sparing Richard the thought that he had spent his money a little foolishly, with what might be a succumbing to cheap effects, who therein sensed a fatherly discipline that one could embrace or be unembraced by, fail or master, as one son or the other did (see **Spin the bottle**).

- In West Germany to work on Cold War missile defense, but in his career not advancing so far as he might for want of a formal degree. Asked whether a Jew felt uneasy in that country, which had so recently cleansed itself of Jews, Joel said that for his ancestors the persecutor had been the czar, to the east, an answer that located anti-Semitism in a foreign past, disengaged with it as unworthy of one's better notion of the world, a view akin to that of the assimilated in Vienna before the war, for whom tragically such ugly evil was beneath conceiving.[83]

[83] Joel's response does not express a true insouciance, but a fine-tuning of Richard's question. On other occasions Joel highlighted anti-Semitism. Having quoted a passage of raw prejudice in a *Perry Mason* novel, he commented, "We've recently been reminded of the U.S.'s late entry into the battle against Hitler; if he'd been smart enough to attack only Jews and Slavs, he surely would have inherited the world" (letter, August 28, 1990).

- The teacher of Joel's laugh, for though it came more lightly and less hysterically, it came quickly like Joel's.

- A weak jaw, shrunken, even deformed, that impeded chewing.

- Napper on the bed, in his underwear, door open, on his back, legs and arms spread straight, his crucifix pose, Joel said.

Prell, Michael. Joel's older brother and **contact person**, an economist, one of the powerful "barons" at the Federal Reserve during Alan Greenspan's tenure.[84] Sometimes you spotted him on C-SPAN, backing up Greenspan in testimony before Congress.

In 1997, the *National Journal* named Michael to its Washington 100 list of the most influential men and women in the federal establishment. He was joined there by Greenspan, the vice president, the attorney general, the secretaries of defense, state, and treasury, the Speaker of the House, two swing-vote Supreme Court justices, and several of the more powerful senators.

[84] Lawrence H. Meyer, *A Term at the Fed: An Insider's View* (New York: HarperCollins, 2004); John Cassidy, "Fleeing the Fed," *New Yorker*, February 19, 1996, 38.

Prell, Ruth Sosin. Joel's mother. Formerly a semiprofessional vocalist whom Joel accompanied at the piano in art song, she took a fatal overdose of **pentobarbital** one month short of her fifty-fifth birthday. She had been reconciled with Joel's father, that is, was living with him again after a separation years before, but suffered crushing headaches that confined her to bed through most of the day. She would emerge from her room at intervals to "zombie around the house," Joel said, with something other than full sympathy and charity.

A family history of suicide is predictive. Her suicide made Joel a motherless son. Suicide became his mother.

Project. May we think about suicide as a construction project or a creative one? Does it have a planning phase and a construction phase like a new apartment complex, or pre- and postproduction like a movie? If Joel envisioned the project (or ratcheted up a plan hatched over decades, if I believe **Barbara**) when his father unexpectedly survived his health crisis, it had several phases, completed over a span of months, and Joel would not have pinpointed the completion date until very near the end. The chosen day was the result of fulfilling all the prior steps: it was time, the final letter in the outline. When the last items of life were disposed of, there was no reason to linger.

My writing about Joel's suicide has been what—A construction? A creative project? A poem? An exercise in failure? A stone I push up the hill only to have it roll down and crush me? A circular story?

I was included in Joel's life and his self-authored ending by virtue of being married to his best friend. Soon after his death I began writing about the change it wrought in me, questioning my role, what I knew and what I didn't know. These questions, I have found, can never be laid to rest. I never absorbed the aftershocks the way Richard did. The material took a shape

within me, like an egg that had been fertilized and was growing, attached to my uterine walls. But it was a shape I failed to
realize again and again. Still, I kept trying, unsure whether the
labor would ever end or just beget another failure.[85]

[85] First formal articulation, "The Substitute Teacher:
Notes of a Suicide," circa 1999–2000. After reading
the draft, my agent wanted addition of qualities I had
decided were not within the scope of my project: she
wanted me to be a coroner and clinician, biographer
and investigative reporter running interviews with the
remaining family members.

Second formal articulation, "Secretary of Death,"
circa 2006. Resurrected, reconceived. This time an
editor suggested fictionalizing Joel so that I could
invent a more interesting character with more exciting
and uplifting plot lines. There would be a dramatic
twist in the story line—he'd meet a woman who
would change his life; a treatment would be found to
control Joel's diabetes and allow him to live a normal
life. There was no end to the possibilities one could
imagine, transforming Joel's story into something
vibrant and pleasing. But I couldn't do it. I felt compelled to tell the truth as best I could, without the
filter of fiction. This felt like an obligation even if it
doomed me to failure.

Questions.

1. Had we understood and acted to stop or dissuade him, might our efforts have made a difference? (For possible answers, see **Plan** and **A tale told by his rabbi, full of sound and fury, etc.**)

2. "He isn't going to kill himself, is he?" (asked of Richard by his mother, upon hearing of Joel's **gifts**, a question I echoed upon receiving Joel's last letter [see **Answering machine**]).

3. Was his project a feat of engineering and science, like a controlled nuclear reaction, constructed with his father's technical prowess? Or was it a performance played with his mother's musical gift?

4. What does one do with the things the dead leave behind?

Reassembly. The day before Joel's departure we dismantled the **bed of metamorphosis** for new carpet to be installed, moving the parts down to the basement. That evening Richard had a meeting to attend, and I raked leaves in the backyard while Joel vacuumed the new carpet. I had not asked him to do so—he volunteered. His neuropathy seemed to leave him weak and short of breath, and he worked at the carpet a long time. Through the bedroom window I could see his stooped figure as he pondered during pauses. I wondered whether he had become lost in his vacuuming, in domestic reverie. Maybe he was thinking about the history of the thing for which he was preparing a place.

Eventually he put the vacuum away and took it upon himself to carry the disassembled bed upstairs from the basement. He could carry only a single component at a time—side piece, headboard, footboard—resting in the bedroom between trips. I was surprised by his endeavor; it was more physical activity than I had seen from him during the visit. He was determined to vacuum the carpet for me and carry up the pieces of the bed, and he performed both tasks ritualistically. His thin flannel shirt grew wet; he panted heavily from his labors. He did not reassemble the bed but stacked the parts neatly against the wall. *He's run out of steam*, I thought.

His methodical procedure was, I realized later, a way of saying good-bye through gestures and objects. Perhaps he intended to prepare the bed for us fully, the bed on which he had best realized his romantic hopes, the bed he had given Richard twenty years before. But some barrier that was not fatigue or weakness or shortness of breath prevented him from fulfilling his intent. Perhaps he had underestimated the sorrows of the task, of fitting together his history and seeing it in complete form. Or he felt it best to leave the bed in parts, as befitting the future soon to unfold. His death would break the circle of our friendship, and making the bed whole must have struck him as fraudulent or impossible. So he stopped short and set the pieces against the wall, like a puzzle for us to sort out.

But we saw nothing in the disassembled parts. The next day Richard put the bed together, and we resumed our life on it. In late October Joel sent a letter in which he apologized for leaving the frame in pieces, fearing his neglect had provoked Richard. After his death, I understood. He had spoken his love and guilt in the language, splintered and stained, of the bed of metamorphosis.

Reception. As we passed through the lobby of the church for the memorial service for Charlie, my neighbor's father, a montage of photographs culled from his childhood, maturity, and old age greeted us. Its bracing centerpiece was a blow-up of the young man with his new wife, who spilled from his arms with unrestrained joy. Inside the sanctuary, friends and family packed into gleaming pews; the filing in of relatives alone took five minutes, they were so numerous, and there was a delay while folding chairs were set up for the overflow. The service itself was of the sort typical nowadays, a celebration of the life of the deceased. If there were domestic squabbles or career disappointments in Charlie's story, they were not portrayed in the words we heard. If he knew despair, loneliness, or pain, if existence is suffering, the Buddha's noble truth, then all that happened in the wings, behind heavy curtains. No body anchored the nave, no casket sleek and dark to brood on.

A substantial reception followed in the rectory, where suntanned great-grandchildren sprawled on the uncomfortable couches, looking too robust and healthy to be corralled inside. After this affair for the benefit of the public crowd, we carpooled to an invited reception at Charlie's house, where slivers of parmesan and smoked salmon were passed on silver trays. The widow never sat down, for she could find no place to do so in a house spilling over with warm wishes, tears of love, and gratitude for Charlie's abundant life.

My own mood, I admit, was a comparative chagrin. Remarking on the profusion of guests with the woman next to me, who held a small plate of fruit she did not touch, we agreed that our own exits would provoke no such send-off. We had traveled too far from where we began, lost too much along the way, made too many disappointments and messes. No generations of family would crowd to the church; no friends from childhood would tell stories of our wit and gaiety. When our time came, there would be no grand hurrah.

For some, the circle is broken. For some, life shrinks in time.

Red-tailed hawk. Over time I have reunited the binoculars to their original purpose and have successfully stood in for Joel as their owner.

When we first moved to the river house, I was purely excited by what I saw outside it. The birds and deer did not speak words I didn't want to hear, like loquacious neighbors, or leave objects behind I could not handle, or so I thought. But beside the ecstasy of wild turkeys that nested in trees, of leisurely deer across the river, there was also death and the premonition of it.

I reach for my binoculars when I want to see what's going on with the mammals and birds. But when I pull them out of their case and feel their cold weight in my hands, I recall that they are meant for Joel. When I glass the landscape, searching out some sign of life, I am looking through fated lenses, like the man in Cormac McCarthy's *The Road*. I am looking through a dead man's eyes.

I have become expert at washing dishes without attending to them, putting plates and cups away while my eyes are pinned to the scene outside the windows. At first maybe I don't see anything unusual. I note how low the river is or how high, flooding the banks and seeping into the woodland, encroaching on the abandoned canoe lolling on its side in the tall grass. Only after looking steadily do I begin to see. On this winter morning of mixed rain and snow, across the river, in an area of soggy woodland, a hawk, a broad-winged, red-tailed hawk, plunges from the sky for prey.

I retrieve my binoculars and raise them to my eyes. The hawk has something in its beak, its talons holding something on the ground, and it has spread its wings facing away, and thrashes its head up and down, rhythmically, ceremonially, until the prey creature clatters apart. The mechanical dance of death goes on a long time. I can't see what the hawk has gotten—its back is to me, its wings spread. The prey has to be big enough to require prolonged killing—no one, two, three and its neck is snapped. No rodent this.

And then I can't watch anymore. I drop the binoculars on the counter on their side by the sink. I leave the hawk to its killing. I have known this moment was coming, have seen it coming toward me for years, the day I would hold the binoculars of the dead man and watch death happen, and we would be one.

Richard. My husband, and Joel's oldest and best friend. The two grew up in L.A. in the fifties and sixties, went to the same schools, walked the same orange-tree streets, became acquainted in a health class at Reseda High School in 1966, talked of girls, later of women, of Bergman and Buñuel, of poetry and education, then of children, and then, much later, of nothing.

Rigor mortis. Achieved. This stiffening of the muscles after death is temporary, lasting up to three days. If Joel's note to the police accurately stated his appointed day of death, his body was in the last hours of rigor mortis when he was found by Officer Cassanego.

River house. Moved into during the trailing years, necessitating an evaluation of things to be transferred from the old house, with its silver maple and arborvitae. The river house is nestled in trees just above and along the Red Cedar River. From every window I see the flow of water and, beyond, the undeveloped woodland on the other bank. Not a game preserve by any means; still, it's a place where humans and animals coexist.

Role. A part defined by a script. Joel could not have considered how hard it would be for us to play the role he wrote for us. Richard's refusal to believe that Joel could have written such a cruel story blinded him to its denouement. See **Gifts**.

Roses. Cultivated by Joel in the backyard of his apartment, loving no one near, roses his only companions in domestic life. "The fragrance of dying roses is a perfume against which even a young girl's hair can't compare."[86]

[86] Letter, July 1983.

Salesman. By March 1979, following his graduation from Berkeley, Joel had a job at Pactel, marketing telephones and telephone service. He took some pride in himself as salesman, talking customers into buying all the phone service they needed.

"Secretary of Death." An unpublished, full-length literary mortography of Joel. I derived its title from John Berger: "Truly we writers are the secretaries of death."[87] When I ask Richard questions about Joel, he often can't answer, doesn't remember. I find it hard to understand the limits of his memory. In contrast, I have a great capacity in retrieving details from the past. Observing and remembering, this is my habitual stance. It's as if I think I'll be called on at an unspecified future date to give testimony and reconstruct a scene before a great tribunal. From an early age, I have thought, *I must remember this.* I must penetrate to the heart of things, to what is being said, to what is animating the action, to the feelings no one will own.

When I've told people I was writing about a friend's suicide, they have assumed a sanitized and glamorized version of Joel—a golden boy. A subject worth writing about must be exceptional, someone who achieved success, became larger than life. The subject of such writing must himself be noteworthy. There is an inherent mystery and curiosity in a person who, seen as successful, ends his life. When the writer Louis Owens shot himself in the chest at the Albuquerque airport, colleagues asked, "How could someone that

[87] John Berger, "Her Secrets," in *The Graywolf Annual Three: Essays, Memories, and Reflections*, ed. Scott Walker (Saint Paul: Graywolf Press, 1986), 6.

successful kill himself?" The subject of suicide has to be different from the humble likes of us. Statesmen, inventors, artists, CEOs, explorers, film stars, writers who left a mark on the world. Someone who amassed a fortune, left behind a monument to his industry and talent.

Suicide, however, is an equal opportunity employer and not choosy about whom it picks. While Joel was smart, curious, creative, a lover of literature and art, funny in a dark bleak kind of way, a gardener and lover of roses, and a devoted teacher for a period of time, he was, looked at through the standard lenses, not a large subject. He was nothing of a golden boy; he was the antigolden boy, a stuck-in-the-mud boy. He wasn't famous. He belonged to the ranks of invisible men in America who perform the poorly rewarded and unrecognized jobs we depend on and who live lives on the brink of erasure. But he did leave a mark.

Joel wasn't a person to like easily, and he had few friends and perhaps no intimates. I wanted to like him; after all, he was my husband's best and oldest friend, and if that wasn't enough motivation, there was his sad family history. But I was never able to penetrate his reserve, his stance of stoic failure and diminished returns. I was never able to pry away the face he presented. He was prickly, not easily pleased by people, those he worked with or encountered casually, the kids he taught. Nothing passed muster, whether it be the gift we gave him or the comment I made while we looked at a painting in a museum. He was, of course, primarily unhappy with himself. When Joel did talk about his life, I felt a tightness in my chest, part guilt, part anger. I felt guilty that my life appeared to be easier than his, and I felt angry that he made me feel guilty about it, made me aware that our lives weren't equally blessed, equally lucky.

And yet, "There is no one to whom one yearns to connect as a person who has committed suicide."[88] Not because he was a golden boy, an important personage, and easy to like. But because he wasn't golden and didn't let me like him. Joel didn't ask me to remember him. He didn't ask me to take a single action to salvage his life from the waste heap of suicide. I just can't help myself.

[88] Andrew Solomon, *The Noonday Demon: An Atlas of Depression* (New York: Simon and Schuster, 2001), 265. In *Haunted Heart: A Biography of Susannah McCorkle*, by Linda Dahl (Ann Arbor: University of Michigan Press, 2006), 287–88 n. 9, this sentence is attributed to Edwin S. Shneidman, *The Suicidal Mind* (New York: Oxford University Press, 1996), but I have been unable to locate it in that volume. Richard, who copyedited the McCorkle biography and as an undergraduate took Shneidman's class on suicide at UCLA, showed the quotation to me, and it became the misattributed epigraph to "Secretary of Death."

Self-accusation. I accuse myself of refusing to connect, to attach myself to the things Joel left us. He cut his ties to things, one object at a time, sending them out into the world, to us. Like Joel, in reverse, I refuse to accept them.

Self-annihilation. Shorthand for systematically destroying points of connection with others.

Self-pity. "It won't surprise you that what's been keeping me from getting a letter to you has been the usual problem of griping and self-pity. Not that griping and self-pity are bad: given something worth griping and pitying oneself about, they're the domes and arches of great letters. In fact, given the way everyone around me seems to be losing their jobs and/or having their life mangled, fabulous letters ought to be arriving there by the bagful. I, on the other hand, having long since abandoned both life and career as goals inappropriate to my abilities, am proof against any misfortunes worthy of gripes or pity."[89]

[89] Letter, June 3, 1991.

Sisyphus. Mythological figure who suffers a human condition. Joel was the substitute teacher, the futile laborer, his students the rock of his impossible uphill climb. He was the modern absurd man.

1635 San Andres Street. A home briefly shared with Gale in Santa Barbara. Joel's descriptions of it were ecstatically rendered dreams of domestic bliss to be. The house was spacious after their student life in an apartment, the neighborhood busy enough to be interesting without too much noise. The front porch looked out on rosebushes, lemon trees, a magnolia, pink lilies, ferns. Joel was rapt in cozy, domestic pleasure over an interior "too wonderful to describe": living room, dining room, a well-equipped kitchen, two bedrooms, newly carpeted or hardwood floors, French windows, built-in china hutches, and glassed bookcases. He was full of plans to make furniture to fill the rooms. Here they set up the **bed of metamorphosis.**

Their residence in the house was short-lived.

Spanish main. In the winter following Joel's death, the **bed of metamorphosis** lay too low to carry me safely through the long nights of grim storm. The foam sagged until my hips touched the plywood foundation that still insisted on natural environments. In the morning after a night of churning seas, my lower back was hot to the touch, for something had lodged there. I went to the doctor, who asked what bed I slept on. How could I begin to answer? I touched on its properties, and the doctor said the bed had to go.

With Richard I broached the subject of a new bed reluctantly. He doesn't like endings. He wanted to sleep on the bed of metamorphosis, and that bed alone, for the rest of his life. He did not want to believe that the bed was broken, nor the friendship, nor the life. But something had shattered, and it couldn't be fixed.

I chose a new bed that differs in every way from the old. The new bed is high; it floats above the fray, a bed of rest. It has a box spring and mattress designed for maximum support. Unlike the dark-stained wood of old, this bed is built of alder, a gold braid of honey, a cradle of light.

The morning the new bed was scheduled for delivery, Richard dismantled the old. He carried the foam mattress and all the pieces but the headboard out to the garage. I was combing my hair in the bathroom doorway when he passed through, the foam struggling out from under his arm. "Say good-bye," he said softly. I thought of what he didn't say. *Good-bye, shape-shifter, where my children were conceived, bed passed from friend to friend, bed on which so many lovers lay that I slept in a crowded grave. Good-bye to what we leave and what leaves us.*

Richard propped the headboard, with its lone Spanish tile, against the silver maple at the front of our yard that had dropped its leaves on Joel's shoulder. Richard taped on a sign: "Free. Ring doorbell for the rest." It was a little pun. I didn't think anyone would take the bed—I thought it had been a bed for the last time. Indeed, no one stopped all that day, until after dinner a young man and a woman wearing a headband knocked on the door to inquire. They looked freshly in love. Richard hauled the components out from the garage, and the young couple loaded the bed—foam and frame, plywood and tile—into their small black pickup and drove its mutability away.

Spectacular suicide. A suicide staged in a landscape of outsize proportions, a sublime setting, publicly noted and recorded; a performed suicide where the place overshadows the act itself and the consequences it leaves in its wake. These dramatic deaths constitute a small percentage of the whole but are inversely noted and mythologized. The Golden Gate Bridge is a public, trafficked place, internationally known as a platform for the spectacular. Suicide from the bridge enters its history, the myth and lore of the city. In this outstanding instance, the location absorbs the act itself and its consequences. The place substitutes for the act, overshadowing the person who jumped and his story.

Spin the bottle. A game of luck with large consequences. Joel referred to it in an analysis of his reasons for choosing the teaching profession:

> I got to thinking about the relationship between me being a teacher and my childhood and arrived at some new insights into my relationship with my father. Memories of how boring it was to be doing things that should have been interesting and instructive had my father only explained the ultimate reason and purpose of my dragging wires under the house; of watching for some light to flash . . . etc. I became aware of a focused resentment that had somehow eluded my consciousness. One thing I don't like about my having been subjected to psychiatry when I should have been playing spin-the-bottle is that I can't avoid coming up with psycho-stories like the following: Feeling that his father had failed as a father, giving over much of his fatherly responsibility to teachers, Joel attacks the father image by having a vasectomy before reaching an age when he might reasonably expect to become a father,[90] and chooses a life emulating and building upon

[90] He had the vasectomy while living with Gale.

his teacher (father-surrogate) models; Joel finds teaching especially significant and involving and emotionally swamping (remember the breakdown a year and some ago) because it is something more or quite different from just teaching and finds the idea of himself being a father virtually unthinkable except when he thinks of adopting a child, something he made moves toward doing when he investigated becoming a Big Brother when he finished school at Berkeley.[91]

Turning into a big brother, not the younger one, was also part of Joel's game (see *The Glory Hole*).

[91] Letter, February 16, 1983.
For the breakdown a year
earlier see **Time travel**.

Spoon altar. My mother collected silver spoons. She had a special
illuminated nook constructed between the kitchen and dining
room where she could hang them, a shrine you'd pass by several times a day. At Christmastime she stood before it, an apron
appliquéd with red poinsettias tied about her waist, polishing
the spoons one by one, checking its reflection of her face, and
hanging each in its spot like a museum piece, an artifact from
Marie Antoinette's scullery. When she had polished them all,
more lovingly than she touched anyone, she stood back to
admire the several spoons now merged into a transubstantial
whole.

They were tiny spoons, hardly large enough to lift a single
raspberry, perhaps two blueberries if they weren't plump. If I
were hungry, in need of food, these spoons would never do.
Passing by the hanging spoons, I was seized with an angry
impulse to yank one down, take it outside, and dig holes, stir
mud pies, perhaps even bury it by the back fence where I alone
could find it.

Why do spoons, however ornate and showy, turned like the
heads of well-bred horses, look so bland? The sun never strikes
a spoon the way it strikes the blade of a knife. A raised spoon
is never lifted above a woman's curtained shoulder, nor does
she bring it down in the house with force. Polished, without

smudges, my mother's spoons suggested a sugarland highway, silver lined, curving to the sea, leading to a world of waves like inverted teacups.

My mother's collection, though unvalued by me, was valuable to someone besides her. Our house was robbed and the silver spoons stolen, to be sold piece by piece or maybe marketed as a collection. Thereafter the illuminated altar of spoons remained vacant and unlit and hosted no communions.

Spoons, commemorative.
In the package that came on November 17 were two commemorative spoons from the Chicago World's Fair of 1933—polished by Joel before he sent them. The front of the stem reads "A Century of Progress," the theme of the Great Exposition at the fair. At the top of the reverse is a reproduction of the Hall of Science. The spoons are worth no more than his **stamp collection**.

Joel did not say how he came by the spoons or why he kept them. He was born in Chicago, as was his mother, who lived there with her family at the time of the fair. Richard learned some of these facts when he sorted through the stamp boxes, having carried them down from the attic in hopes of assembling a chronology, of understanding Joel's life and making an order of his death. Richard worked through the empty envelopes and found among those with postage from foreign countries an envelope mailed from Ohio. It turned out to be the one item of value to us in the collection, an item Joel would never have let us see had he known that the envelope still contained its letter. It had escaped his rage to order and dispose, to cruelly conceal from us his plot to end his life. I cherish the letter, as a crack of light through the black shutter he drew down between us. It was written by Gale, with whom he lived during the brief years of his best chances, and was sent in the first days of their romance. The letter says, "To realize that you love me, too, is a prayer come true."

At first we kept the spoons with the other items that arrived in the final package. Later we thought we'd try to use the spoons, and mixed them in with others in the silverware tray. There you find the remains of Richard's bachelor-days tableware, a scattered set my mother no longer wanted, cheap store-bought spoons we added as others were lost at the park or fell into garbage disposals. But it turns out that we always choose other spoons with which to eat our ice cream or oatmeal. I have never polished Joel's spoons and don't know if I ever will. If I can ever bring myself to lift one to my lips, I'd prefer the taste of tarnish, bitter and lingering, and proper to my life-beclouded eye.

Stamp collection. Joel was the son of a collector and inherited a
collector's impulses, manifested most fully in the form of raw
accumulation. In childhood he began a collection of stamps,
then abandoned it, but never disposed of those he had gathered. In his midtwenties he was still saving exotic stamps,
usually those sent from foreign countries, by keeping the
envelopes to which they were attached. Two decades later, a
few weeks after his last visit and a few weeks before he shot
himself, he sent us this collection, two boxes of stamps and

envelopes, requiring FedEx to obtain a signature before delivering them into our possession.

I don't know if he believed the collection valuable or imagined our children might carry it forward as a matter of fun. But neither of them showed an interest. They liked to gather rocks or shells and sometimes joined in collecting fads—Beanie Babies, Pokémon cards—but it was the fever of the fad that mattered, and soon it burned out. Although the stamps lit no flame in our kids, they were Joel's penultimate bequest and left us perplexed. Should we view the collection as a connection to his final days, an extension of him? Could we, by continuing the collection, continue his life, at least as an act of loyalty? Were we disloyal if we did not keep it? After poring over the boxes and wondering where we'd store them and why, we decided to have them appraised, thinking we could put aside the proceeds, perhaps toward our kids' college education. Richard took the stamps to a dealer, who set the two boxes on a table, flipped through them efficiently—this took maybe a minute—and announced that it was common stuff. He punched some numbers on his hand calculator and offered $23.71 for the whole batch—less than Joel's costs in shipping the stamps to us. Richard hesitated. To sell them for that amount would be a disgrace. On the other hand, what good were these musty boxes? In the end, Richard brought them home and hauled them up to the attic.

About this choice of spot for long-term storage of the stamps I will say that it's something of a climb to get up there. The boxes ascended in stages over several days, from the living room to a second-story base camp, down a hallway, through a bedroom, and then—here's where the real obstacles lie—up a narrow stairway that is usually clogged with sleeping bags, summer fans, folding chairs, Christmas decorations, and other seasonal items that have never reached the summit. Besides seasonal items, the attic is the spot for cluttering items—and all the feelings they provoke—that we do not use but do not want to get rid of: drafts of abandoned novels, forgotten diaries, children's art projects, old Halloween costumes with plumed and iridescent masks, valentines, love letters, baby clothes. (When you get to the top of the attic stairs, skeletons may pour down, unhinged by the human presence ascending from the living world below.) It was among this latter group that the stamps found their rest, and it was then that their status as collection, in jeopardy ever since Joel as a child ceased his systematic attention to them, collapsed. They were now rubble in boxes and located in our house among that which we cannot dispose of.

Steinway Model K. Tall black upright crypt, purchased with proceeds from a CalSTRS lump-sum payout, Richard being Joel's named beneficiary.

At the time of Joel's last visit we had a spinet. He played, sitting down in a moment when we were busy with our tasks and he had time to touch some chords of a piece I could not name, contemplative and gentle, a beautiful surprise of music in the midafternoon.

The music moved me, and I left what I was doing—folding laundry, I think—to listen more closely. At my appearance in the doorway Joel stopped.

"Oh, don't stop," I said. "You play so beautifully."

He did not resume but got up from the piano as if to leave the room.

"Do you practice much at home?" I asked.

He hedged, then mumbled about the difficulty with his fingers, which could no longer feel the keys.

He spoke directly, however, about the piano, saying that we should replace it with a better instrument. He had listened to our daughter play; she had reached a stage at which she needed to hear a truer sound, he said.

When Joel's father sent claim forms showing that Richard was the beneficiary of Joel's retirement account, we chose the rebuilt Steinway as an appropriate purchase with which to honor his bequest.

It turned out that Richard had misread the forms, and there was only enough in the account for a down payment. We took out a loan for the rest.

Story. "It is . . . characteristic that not only a man's knowledge or wisdom, but above all his real life—and this is the stuff that stories are made of—first assumes transmissible form at the moment of his death. Just as a sequence of images is set in motion inside a man as his life comes to an end—unfolding the views of himself under which he has encountered himself without being aware of it—suddenly in his expressions and looks the unforgettable emerges and imparts to everything that concerned him that authority which even the poorest wretch in dying possesses for the living around him. This authority is at the very source of the story. . . . Death is the sanction of everything that the storyteller can tell."[92]

[92] Walter Benjamin, *Illuminations*, ed. Hannah Arendt, trans. Harry Zohn (New York: Schocken, 1986), 94.

Substitute. (1) A person who takes the place of or acts instead of; (2) something that is put in place of something else or is available for use instead of something else; (3) something cheaper or inferior that is used instead of a standard article; (4) an artificial product used to replace a natural one; (5) a word or grammatical feature that replaces another word, a phrase, or a clause, in a context; (6) a special tool or part used in place of a regular tool.

Substitute teacher. A name of failure.

> They move from school to school.
> A bit of this, a bit of that,
> A public relations envoy
> Performer, model, preacher,
> Policeman, translator, counselor, advisor,
> Salesman, diplomat, ambassador, cleaning person,
> Mapmaker and artist, historian, friend, computer expert,
> Juggler, rainmaker, doormat.
>
> He takes the place of the real thing.
> He stands in for the teacher, a dike
> Between the students and the abyss.
> He has no homeroom.
>
> He performs substitution,
> Models how to be replaceable.

Joel did not wear lightly his status as a substitute teacher. Substitution became the sign of who he was, his position in society. He thought that only someone like himself, sloughing in the trenches of public school teaching—and worse, subbing—could ever know teaching. He once responded with a sneer to Richard's reference to teaching as an honorable profession: "I don't consider teaching at present to be an honorable profession. In fact, I no longer ask to be recognized as a 'real teacher' rather than 'just a substitute.'"[93]

[93] Letter, September 27, 1988.

Suicide. An act that names the actor; an act that creates a mystery, a gap between the promise and the outcome, between the person we thought we knew and the person who decided to die. The forbidden. The dark secret disrupting the family seams. The exposure of a gaping hole no one wants to see. The refusal our lives repress.

"Suicide." A poem. Or should I call it performance art?

Albert Camus, the great philosopher of suicide, recognized the aesthetic quality of certain deaths of this sort: "An act like this is prepared within the silence of the heart, as is a great work of art."[94]

[94] Camus, *The Myth of Sisyphus*, 4.

Suicide Intent Scale. All the signs of Joel's intent were there, a textbook case, as if he had sent us a checklist. I was too stupid, too passive, too endlessly deferring to glance at it.

The Suicide Intent Scale was developed by Aaron T. Beck and colleagues to measure the seriousness of attempts at suicide—the intensity of the intent.[95] Under each of eight headings, one can score zero, one, or two points; the higher the score, the greater the seriousness of the attempt. Joel's perfect total score of 16, could I have administered to him a questionnaire, would have indicated a perfect risk.

		COMMENT
A. Isolation		
0. Somebody present		
1. Somebody nearby, or in visual or vocal contact		
2. No one nearby or in visual or vocal contact	✓	*Alone in windowless bathroom*
B. Timing		
0. Intervention is probable		
1. Intervention is not likely		
2. Intervention is highly unlikely	✓	*No one ever visited*

(CONTINUED ON FOLLOWING PAGE)

		COMMENT
C. Precautions against discovery/intervention		
0. No precautions		
1. Passive precautions (as avoiding others but doing nothing to prevent their intervention; alone in a room with an unlocked door)		
2. Active precautions (as in a locked door)	✓	
D. Acting to get help during/after attempt		
0. Notified potential helper regarding attempt		
1. Contacted but did not specifically notify potential helper regarding attempt		
2. Did not contact or notify potential helper	✓	Kept secret from all
E. Final acts in anticipation of death (e.g., will, gifts, insurance)		
0. None		
1. Thought about or made some arrangement		
2. Made definite plans or completed arrangements	✓	Disposed of all belongings, etc.
F. Active preparation for attempt		
0. None		
1. Minimal to moderate		
2. Extensive	✓	"Hatched a perfect plan (over decades, probably)—everything was handled to the last detail."
G. Suicide note		
0. Absence of note		
1. Note written, but torn up; note thought about		
2. Presence of note	✓	Letter to police
H. Overt communication of intent before the attempt		
0. None		
1. Equivocal communication		
2. Unequivocal communication	✓	"On or before Friday, November 17, I will have taken my own life using my .38 revolver."

One has to wonder how I saw so little about someone with a perfect score. Maybe I thought, below my thoughts, that Joel had a right to do with his life what he wanted, even if it meant denying that life's very conditions. Or I preferred to protect myself—from what? From the face of death beneath the mask? From having to exert myself on his behalf? The answers I can offer do not defend me.

95 I have modified this scale from the version reproduced in Kay Redfield Jamison, *Night Falls Fast* (New York: Vintage, 2000), 40–44.

Suicide note. Last written words of the dead. Perhaps one-fifth of suicides are accompanied by a note. In style and form these final words seem to refuse all of the patterns that define literary genres. Some are written to ease the pain of survivors, some to hone their pain; some explain the reasons for the desperate act, while others leave practical instructions for the disposition of bodily remains and belongings. Some notes are fully human—full of human limitation, rotting with imperfection, half-baked ideas, self-pity, illusion, self-importance, simpering sentimentality, impulsive anger, unhealed wounds. Some notes are banal ("I have taken my life in order to provide capital for you");[96] some are desperate with love. The mood may be generous (Virginia Woolf's tender words for Leonard) or bitter ("Goodbye you old prick").[97]

Joel's suicide note was sent to the police, alerting them to his plan and providing the data and tools required to recover his body. Perhaps two days before he died, Joel mailed a manila envelope to the Investigations Bureau of the police station on Bryant Street. It was opened on the afternoon of November 20, 1995, by Inspector Heller, No. 1608 in Operations. Inside was a typed letter, a key to Joel's apartment, and his driver's license. The letter stated, "On or before

[96] Marc Etkind, . . . Or Not to Be: A Collection of Suicide Notes (New York: Riverhead Books, 1997), 33.

[97] Etkind, Or Not to Be, 10.

Friday, November 17, I will have taken my own life using my .38 revolver." The impersonality of this note is a signature of sorts. It tells us that his death was planned to the last detail. It tells us Joel didn't think he'd be discovered in the normal course of events. No one would be disturbed by a ringing phone that wasn't answered. He felt a sense of mastery: he was in charge of his own death and cool in its contemplation. He didn't like sloppy emotionalism, inconsiderate impulsiveness. Joel's note tells us that he couldn't abide more failure. He didn't want to botch his departure from life as he had botched its living.

Synecdoche. Rhetorical figure of substitution, part for a whole. Suicide substitutes for his life, a trope through which life is represented.

A tale told by his rabbi, full of sound and fury, etc. A young boy had been sent to the grocery store to pick up some essential doodads for lunch. Minutes, under the influence of the additive property, became larger and larger fractions of an hour, and the boy's mother became increasingly concerned. Just as her concern teetered on the brink of worry, the boy arrived, apparently unharmed.

"I was getting worried," said the young boy's mother. "Where have you been?"

"I'm sorry," said the boy. "I went straight to the market, but on the way back, there was this little kid, and he was crying because his tricycle was busted up. So I stopped to help him."

A bit surprised and curious now, the boy's mother asked, "How could you help? You don't know anything about fixing tricycles."

"Right. So I sat down next to the kid and helped him cry."[98]

[98] Letter, November 22, 1984.

Telescope. In June of the year before his last visit, as a birthday present to our children, Joel sent his old telescope, largely disassembled, with a four-inch parabolic mirror and an equatorial mount, complete with a diagram and note containing useful pointers, such as "Do not ever look at the sun." The note was signed in Vulcan: "Live long and prosper."

The telescope arrived damaged, its long tube dented and the lenses out of whack. It went to storage in the attic for some years, but eventually Richard dragged it to the curb and affixed a sign saying "Free," in hopes that someone who knew telescopes would rescue and repair it. The telescope was gone within an hour.

Test. Was Joel testing us to see what we would and would not notice? Joel once gave such a test to Richard, who did not know he was being tested; Joel then announced to Richard that he had failed. First Richard failed the test, the contents of which were never disclosed, and then Joel presented Richard with his failure, a failure that could never be remedied. Did we fail the test of love?

Thanksgiving. Holiday that followed the news of Joel's death, ours entwined with him, as his with us: "Thanksgiving never meant anything to me until your family and Gale endowed the concept with its proper significance."[99]

Late afternoon on Wednesday we were playing loud music, as we often do when we are in a flurry of cooking and cleaning for company. The windows vibrated with the bass guitar. We had just come home from the market, and Richard was putting groceries away. I had begun to vacuum the still-new carpet in the bedroom when the phone rang. I barely heard it. Richard answered and disappeared into the basement to talk away from the noise. I continued vacuuming, in a cleaning reverie. Having finished, I came out of the bedroom and saw Richard. The guitars were very loud and he tried to say something—his mouth was moving—but I couldn't hear him. He looked distraught, colorless, standing under the arched entry to the dining room. He signaled that he was going to turn off the music.

When Richard returned he said, "He did it."

At first I didn't catch on. "Who did what?"

"He killed himself. That was Joel's father on the phone."

This is how the news hits—when we're merrily engaged in a consuming task, like baking a pie or folding our socks or sucking up fuzz.

---

[99] Letter, November 1975.

Timeline. A chronological ordering of events. In an effort to understand what had happened and to find the story, Richard constructed a table that began with the building of a Steinway in 1908 and ended with Gale's letter of August 30, 1996, in which she said that she was unsurprised by the news of Joel's death.

The timeline took the form of entries in two columns. Some examples on the theme of parents:

Card to Joel and Gale from his mother: "Dear Chicks"	September 22, 1973

and

"That Joel! I think it's about time he 'found' himself."	Letter from R's mother, December 6, 1982

and

Thinks of calling R's mother on Mother's Day	May 1983

and (to add a little levity)

His father is going to   June 2, 1984
marry Marilyn. Quotes a
student paper: "Capital
Punishment should be
abolished because NO one
person should have the
right to kill anyone not
even there selfs."

Time travel. "At the hospital, after some tests, I was diagnosed as suffering from 'stress.' During the next week I diagnosed myself 'bonkers,' and the psychiatrist at Kaiser subsequently diagnosed an 'identity crisis.' I think I prefer my own diagnosis since 'bonkers' captures more of the character of my condition: I spent almost two weeks never really certain in what decade I would find myself the next moment. Rather like the Illustrated Man, I found my life history opening up and displacing me all day long. At times it was so intense that I would be startled finding myself as a teacher standing in front of a classroom full of students when I thought I was in a playground in North Hollywood in 1953. One day of such surprises, one after another, is quite a strain; a whole week of them just about undid me."[100]

[100] Letter, February 20, 1982.

Toast. Delivered in an e-mail from Gale to Richard:

> Were we closer in proximity, we'd raise a glass in memory
> of Joel and swap funny and sad stories of memories of
> Joel. As second best, here's a toast to Joel, on the first
> anniversary of his death. He has been much on my mind
> these last few days. . . . I usually make the 45 minute drive
> into work in the dark, but today was later and I got to
> watch the sunrise on the trip. The sun rises and sets in
> this part of the world with majestic shows. I have to give
> Minnesota a "10" for the glory of the sunrises/sunsets,
> especially in the winter. And I wonder how life can be so
> unbearable that the sunrise isn't enough anymore . . . the
> music of John Coltrane, old Woody Allen films, violin con-
> certi, hockey games and popcorn and being rowdy, beer
> with friends in front of a roaring fire, cross country skiing
> on a cold morning when the only sound is the sshhh of the
> skis on frozen snow, laughing, sleeping in on rainy days or
> staying in on rainy nights, driving with the top down . . . to
> leave this admittedly imperfect life willingly is so hard to
> comprehend. I wonder if the thread here is relationships
> (this might be, as my 15-year-old would say, a chick thing).
> Joel's death certificate says never married. Is this true?

Not that marriage or not is a defining factor in a person's wholeness, but I can only hope that there were (was) relationships that gave Joel some comfort along the way.

I know, unless Joel had changed drastically in the past years, that the friendship you shared with him was a rock. You had a motorcycle once, and I have a vivid snapshot in my memory of you giving Joel a ride on it—You had longish hair and your hair was blowing back, and Joel was sitting on the back as you turned a corner, with his head thrown back and laughing. I remember, too, how once you were in Europe and had fallen in love, and Joel was almost grieving that he had lost you as a friend. He obsessed about it, and no amount of assurance on my part made a difference . . . and then, another letter came from you and, whatever it said, the panic was gone. I think he knew then that distance, loves, jobs couldn't break what the two of you shared. I hope you find some comfort in knowing you were friends.

I had hoped to make a kind of pilgrimage to Colma during this time, but duties and cash flow have made it impossible. So, instead, I've bought myself some flowers and will have a glass of wine tonight for him. I hope you can find a way for a small celebration of Joel, too.
Gale

Tools not elsewhere inventoried and not forgotten. Phillips and flat-blade, stubby, medium, and long screwdrivers, rechargeable battery-powered screwdriver with attachments, ratchet handle with attachment bits and blade, drill motor and drill bits and attachments, small socket wrench and sockets, box wrenches, open-end wrenches, L-shaped rule, 24-inch level, chisels, flat-nose pliers, locking pliers, needle-nose pliers, assorted files, plane.

Truth. Siren song that haunts the aftermath. "My mother's suicide note told my father that she loved him: she lied. I guess suicide is not a great moment of truth after all."[101]

[101] Letter, December 13, 1975.

Unclaimed Baggage Center. In Alabama, a warehouse full of items left behind by travelers. The baggage has stayed unclaimed, and no one knows why. Employees sort through suitcases and duffel bags, tasked with determining what to keep, what to throw away, and how to price the salvageable. When they find a life neatly folded inside an overnight case, they sigh a deep collective sigh, the beginning of a wonder that will never end: What were the lives in which these possessions had a part? Brand-new clothes for a seaside holiday, the delicate white things of a honeymoon, a threadbare sweater, a baby's tiny socks. The employees draw a portrait of the owner, then mourn the portrait and sort the baggage, sending some items to the trash heap, some to the Unclaimed Baggage Center, where a stranger can pick up a fine gold watch for a song. See **Questions**.

The underlying, unifying principle of a life. Into his great see-saw letter of April 1995 Joel dropped, with pretended nonchalance, a paragraph about a moment of profound revelation:

> For honesty's sake, and for the sake of adding a few words, I confess to having achieved a really significant self-analytical breakthrough. I've been having some extraordinary dreams, unlike any I can recall, involving themes of evolution, self-identity, and death; but these have nothing to do with my new understanding. It came to me as I was tidying-up a drawer or two, which involved trying to put my photos into some kind of order. I was looking at these pictures, some of them from the Utah years, some from much earlier, and what you said when I mentioned I couldn't remember what I'd been doing (I don't remember what I was talking about, but it doesn't matter) flashed into my mind and ignited a blazing insight: I was chasing women, you said. That was the key! I'm afraid you're going to have to wait until we can get together, but I've got four or five photos that make it all clear. It's a revelation at last to see the underlying, unifying principle of a life . . . mine, in particular. How can I have missed it for so long? No matter: what matters is that the deepest, most secret pits

of my psyche have been drained, and that's one less thing to worry about anymore.[102]

He never showed us the photos that make it all clear, and I doubt he would ever have permitted entry to that sanctum of privacy. But his intent in April to show them, regardless of how seriously I take it, is evidence that he was still planning to live a while, whereas soon enough he was determined to die, and so destroyed these mementos and all the others (see **World's Fair**).

As a consequence, I do not know what the revelatory principle of his life was. He does not say that chasing women was the principle—though it may have been—only that Richard's barb was the match that lit the blazing insight.

It does not matter, in some sense, what the principle was. Were he to say to me, "This is the truth of my life," I would not believe him. It is not that I would doubt his sincerity or self-awareness or deny the photographic data. It is that there can be no final truth of a life, for such a summary can be formulated only from a perspective that is not life's, an unhuman retrospective on that which is finished. For what is life is a new hour, unprofaned by the past.[103]

Yet I admire the cold bravery of his self-assessment. It is not final, but it is very late, later than late autumn, late as the last slow chord of the orchestra that echoes away. "Nothing doesn't worry me," he says in the April letter.[104] He means the nothing of the void. The nothing after the end.

I do not like to be photographed. My efforts to form a natural smile in front of a lens produce unnatural results, with tensed teeth and tight

---

[102] Letter, April 19, 1995.

[103] "That man who does not believe that each day contains an earlier, more sacred, and auroral hour than he has yet profaned, has despaired of life, and is pursing a descending and darkening way" (Thoreau, *Walden*, 1:141).

[104] He wasn't being ungrammatical or uncouth in this sentence. He might have written, for example, the more obviously proper "Nothingness doesn't worry me." However, a former philosophy major, he likely thought the word *nothingness* implies somethingness, as in Sartre. Joel wanted the idea of *nothing*.

wide eyes like a startled horse. I do best when someone else is sharing the camera's attention, when the subject is the scene, the assembled family or friends or companions, and not myself alone, observed, scrutinized, examined, exposed.

Joel was like me in his unease before the camera. We do not have many photos of him, only eight or ten or so: a young man sitting at a dinette with Richard in Sherman Oaks, a hirsute student on the couch in his Berkeley apartment, a visitor in our living room in Seattle, a subject cajoled into a pose before a rosebush in his backyard. It is not much of a sample from which to draw conclusions, but generally he looks relaxed and cheerful with others, and when framed alone is self-conscious and awkward in posture, arms skewed and head angled to pull away from the lens.

Richard took two photos during the last visit. In one of them Joel, Clare, Larry, and I are loosely gathered, disorderly, scarcely held together by the frame, on the school grounds where Clare had played a soccer match. We were absorbing Joel into the modest pleasures of our mundane life, we thought. Though he is but one person of several in the picture, Joel looks distressed, facing ninety degrees from front, his lips pursed and eyes squinted, his hand unrelaxed in the pocket of his jacket. He must have considered the import of the moment: this photograph would be a document that we would pore over in the future, as proof of the perpetration of a fraud.

The other photo shows Joel alone in our upstairs hallway, caught before he could assume a formal stance. He faces the camera directly this time, but his eyelids are lowered, and it is easy to see in his wry expression an awareness that he was the audience for a play in which we spouted the dialogue of fools. But maybe I imagine his look and it is only the framing assumption, my determination to see his wry awareness, that makes me imagine it.

I could put this question to a test with the Pepper photo sent by **Barbara**. For I do not know when it was taken, whether in the late summer of his last year, as his long plan was nearing consummation, or in a prior time, before he had chosen to die. I should be able to date the Pepper photo by the wryness of Joel's eyes. But I do not think I will try.

Vise. Gripper on and of, a converter of prepositions, a transferor of stability. It holds firmly to the

earth a rubbled piece of world to be worked on.

The powerful vises Joel delivered are Stanley No. 700s, likely obtained from his father. Richard used them to build a garden border out of pressure-treated two-by-twos, framing a place in the little light on the west side of the river house where I had faith to plant shade-tolerant hostas, to be seen beneath the screened porch, or to grow as candy for the fawns.

Voice of authority. Suicide is born from a feeling of guilt that no punishment has attenuated. —PRIMO LEVI

Why. A story we need to hear.

World's Fair. What were the types of things Joel gave us, and what were the types of things he didn't give us?

None of the things he gave us were mementos, intimate souvenirs, signs of his life history: these were destroyed. Letters, photos, his personal papers, that which would reveal him, document his humanness, his struggles as a son, a brother, a friend, a lover, a man: these were destroyed. Signs of his rites of passage, degrees and certificates, records of tests passed, the "compendium which is an autobiography":[105] these were destroyed. They had to be destroyed because they were too revealing: "Because of its connection to biography and its place in constituting the notion of the individual life, the memento becomes emblematic of the worth of that life and of the self's capacity to generate worthiness."[106]

Every item that measured the worth of his life was destroyed—except his letters, which were in our hands. Had he been able, he would have erased that connection, too. But he couldn't ask for their return without tipping us off. And so the letters, documenting his connection to us and to others, the

[105] Susan Stewart, *On Longing: Narratives of the Miniature, the Gigantic, the Souvenir, the Collection* (Baltimore: Johns Hopkins University Press, 1984), 139.

[106] Stewart, *On Longing*, 139.

worth of his life, are still alive in our life, resisting his wish to have them vanish.

All of the items he gave us, then, were *nonmementos*. But he did not give us all of his nonmementos. The bulk of such stuff he got rid of, much of it junk: a stiffened ten-cent paperback from the Goodwill store or an unabsorbent old hand towel. But not all was worthless—he had recordings of the *Ring* cycle and Bach, for example. Why see certain objects into our hands? Why not give them to the Salvation Army, put them out on the street, throw them into the trash? It was hard work to haul them two thousand miles by car, when he could have carried them out to the curb. Why transport them? What made them worth that effort? What distinguished the nonmementos he gave us from the nonmementos he didn't give us?

The objects he transported by car across the country and delivered in person were items of utility: tools, his computer, binoculars and microscope, reference books. All of these objects, with one exception,[107] were useful nonmementos.

Their common nature subjected them, once in our hands, to a common fate: that which is worth having only because it is useful turns worthless when it becomes useless. Unless we treated them as memorabilia, Joel's things were subject to superannuation through wear or damage or advances in technology. The **telescope** never worked. The transformer in the light source for the microscope soon burned out, and the microscope, encrypted in its blond coffin of a box, awaits an unknown fate in the basement storage room. The computer was outmoded by faster chips and bigger drives; the corded drill gave way to a cordless model; the reference books, though they still sit on the bookshelf, have been endusted by the Internet. Only the binoculars and a few of the hand tools have escaped this decay by remaining useful. The tools have been

---

[107] Philip Larkin's *Collected Poems*.

naturalized: Joel's pliers are kept in our toolbox, his screwdrivers in a rack with others, and Richard is unable, he claims, to remember which is which. Only the binoculars retain their charge.

The final things to be inventoried here were in the two shipments that arrived after Joel's last visit: the stamps, the egg coddler, and the spoons. The stamp boxes were for a while a useful source of information but have since returned to limbo, with a destiny much like the microscope's.

That leaves the egg coddler and spoons. Although these items pretend to be useful, they are not. A narrative is attached to them, but I do not know it. The spoons were likely passed to Joel by a family member who attended the World's Fair. The history of how we've come by these things writes over Joel's invisible history with them. Our history is his suicide and our involuntary role in its performance.

These objects stand in for that lost life, and so far I have been unable to awaken them to a new life, a new purpose. They remain oriented toward the past, an assemblage, not a collection in which I can see my own reflection. But their connection to Joel grants them potential as souvenirs.[108] I think I am ready to remove the spoons from the silverware tray, where they have failed as items of use, and place them beside the egg coddler on the shelf in my study. The ensemble will be a small collection of memorabilia, like a setting for a foreign culture's breakfast on display at a world's fair. Or points within a constellation of Joelean objects that no longer burns my eyes. Or a welcome to a friend for a shared meal and the giving of thanks.

[108] "We need and desire souvenirs of events that are reportable, events whose materiality has escaped us, events that thereby exist only through the invention of narrative. . . . The souvenir speaks to a context of origin through a language of longing, for it is not an object arising out of need or use value; it is an object arising out of the necessarily insatiable demands of nostalgia. The souvenir generates a narrative which reaches only 'behind,' spiraling in a continually inward movement rather than outward toward the future" (Stewart, On Longing, 135).

X-ray. A packet of obstructed vision. When Richard moved out of the apartment they shared in San Francisco, Joel was still searching for a permanent teaching position. He moved in with a radiologist who had a room to rent. A note about him shows the trademarks of Joel's style, humor mixed with bitterness: "It's 6:50, Vince has just risen from his mattress of comfortable crumbled dollar bills, his untroubled bed of X-ray futures, and I am again, unemployed and bitter. And angry at myself for having come up with no alternatives. I continue to think of tutoring, but I don't have any clear idea of what or how I should tutor: obviously, from this sentence, I should avoid grammar."[109]

[109] Letter, October 9, 1980.

Years, under the influence of the additive property. Tales of
ghosts and legends of hangings in Abiquiu, New Mexico:
Ghost Ranch. Georgia O'Keefe painted there, and her ashes
were scattered at a spot not publicly known. On the walk back
to Box Canyon, gravesites of those affiliated with the ranch are
camouflaged from the observer by sage and rock. This infor-
mal burial ground faces Pedernal, the rock bluff and spiritual
landmark that O'Keefe painted so many times she believed she
had earned it from God.

When one of the ranch horses is ready to die, a wrangler
takes it out on the range, administers a mortal shot of **pentobarbital**, and leaves the corpse for the coyotes. One wrangler told
me she wants nothing more for herself. At the ranch there are
more bones than flowers. Skulls bleached by the sun hang in
doorways all over Abiquiu, and I have brought home a cow's
skull to mount over my bed, with a chile ristra hanging from
each horn. My dogs regard the skull respectfully, keeping a
watchful eye, and many people find the skull gruesome. They
believe skulls belong outside the house, that I have trans-
gressed an important boundary by bringing one inside, by
making it a part of an intimate space. Yet the skull comforts
me, unites me to horse and steer and even to the animal who
is human. The skull is not a trophy or decorative accessory. I

hang it to remind myself that death needn't happen offstage, in the wings, for someone else.

At Ghost Ranch I found a place where I would have liked Joel to be buried. It's a small sanctuary, called La Resolana (reflected sunlight), on the south side of a building between the main meeting hall and the living quarters, with clay walls, adobe-style, protected from the wind, open to the sky, to the strong sun and the full moon. People pass it many times a day, coming and going. Anyone can easily get to the spot; no horse is required. Residents and visitors gather there to exchange news and share stories. The only bell on the ranch, which rings worship services and storm warnings, hangs in a port in the back wall; the blue sky can be seen through and behind the bell, its thick pull rope hanging down the wall.

In the center of the flagstone floor, a garden. A garden of the flowers of the high desert, drought-resistant, rough and hardy, the earthy growth of the archaic funeral rites for a vegetation god. These flowers tend to themselves and withstand the unrelenting sun. Under the desert skies and sun, the plants grow bountiful, spilling over the bounded area, stems and colors mixing bold golds with softer pinks. A strong plot of color—so deep are the colors that stop the passerby, they have power to hurt. Tucked in the lavish tumble of blooms a marker says, *In remembrance*.

I had no rights to say where Joel would be disposed; that was for his father to say. But I have rights to where I imagine him, what I do to keep myself alive and lay him to rest, to sit down next to him and help him die. I would not cast the dead as far from the living and visit him rarely, give death to the undertakers. I inter him at La Resolana. I say again: even though Joel did his best to die in an empty corner, to write over his life with suicide, I refuse to erase his name from love's ledger. *In remembrance. Joel Lawrence Prell.*

Yes, this is my time. All done. All gone. It's finished. All ready. Complete. Note to police, key. No doubts. Certainty. Deep breath. Now.

So quiet. No sounds. Gun here on the counter. Box of shells here. Unsnap case, slide gun out. Set it on counter, gentle. Slide box open. Tremor in hands. One bullet. Fingertips numb. Slide box shut. Bullet into chamber, as before. There, all the way in, firmly. Flip chamber shut. Click. Locked in, good, as it should be. A good device, good tool. Exact, precise, clean.

Ready. Safety pushes all the way up. Push safety all the way up. That's it. Ready.

Stand? Kneel. Kneel down. Pop in my knee. Tiles hard. My knees, floor hard on my knees. Head up, steady.

How easy. *Easy.* Nothing doesn't worry me. Peace. Yes, *peace.* Deep breath. Peace. They will understand. It was best. You will understand.

No sounds. No hum from the fridge. Extraordinary silence.

Arm up. Muzzle there. A little lower. There. Firmly, don't let it slide. It's hard, like . . . like a muzzle. Steady. Level. The trigger pulls smooth, firm. Steady squeeze, as before.

Will fall. Will fall that way. Leave room. Arm down, slide knees left. There. Good.

Eyes down. No mirror. How easy. Calm. Drawer handle. Wall.

Arm up, muzzle there, again. Peace. Level, steady. Peace. Breathe. Breathe steady. Deep breath. Squeeze steady steady. Peace supreme nothing doesn't

Young manhood. Years of feeling. Living was not yet done with him, and he was not done with living. His life and letters were messy with cries and witticisms and excoriations. But this paradoxical letter, written in the bad month October 1974, was very brief and neat:

> Dear Richard,
>   I hate everything.
> Love,
> Joel

He typed the letter—except his name, signed in red ink.

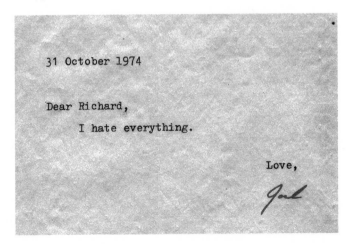

Z, omega, taw. The shoreline of Lake Huron near the tip of Michigan's Lower Peninsula is the haunt of bald eagles, attracted by the joint presence of forest for nests and lake for prey, and perhaps by the common winds to ride on. On that shore I have spotted only juveniles, whose plumage lacks the white cap and tail that mark the mature birds. They are fully adult in size, however, and of a brown so dark that from a ground-bound view it appears black, with strips of white on the underwing, mottled irregularly as if by disease or rot. More ominous than the imperious national symbol with its snow-capped head, these giant flying shadows are like raven heralds sent for us by death.[110]

Some authorities say the eagles see four times as well as a person with perfect vision, some say eight times as well, but I can't comprehend what it would be to possess such power-ful eyes. It is said that they can spot prey a mile away. They can traverse the shore and fly from sight in seconds, but at certain moments near dusk the treetops will unfold a dark-bodied shape with wings as big as a man, its talons and beak an unliv-ing sheen, who pumps the empty light and floats to pause on the axis of my head. He suspends himself on unbeating wings two

[110] "Heraldos negros que nos manda la Muerte" (César Vallejo, The Complete Poetry, ed. and trans. Clayton Eshleman [Berkeley: University of California Press, 2007], 24).

hundred feet above the beach, so close that I can catch his rigid eyes, whose stare has a strength I cannot live in. As he hovers above and I stand under, he peers into every flaw and wrinkle on my face. His eyes shoot arrows of adrenalin into my heart and summon me to their world and inhuman view. Within his gaze, though not in fear, the heartpound says, *My body-strength is gone and I am awe.* I see the sublime, but more, the sublime sees me.

It is the closest I will get in this life to the mystic's vision of the rose and corn of paradise.[111] Or to a final man with rigorous eyes who says, *Yes, this is my time. You will understand.*

[111] "In form then of a pure white rose the saintly host was shown to me" (Dante, *Paradiso*, trans. Charles S. Singleton [Princeton: Princeton University Press, 1975], 21:1–2). See **Apartment, Bathroom (1), Colma, Disposition of the body, Domestic past, Garage sale, Gas, Roses, "Secretary of Death," 1635 San Andres Street,** and **The underlying, unifying principle of a life**. "Although the Master of Life did not allow Lalawethika to enter heaven, he was allowed to gaze upon a paradise, which he described as 'a rich, fertile country, abounding in game, fish, pleasant hunting grounds and fine corn fields'" (R. David Edmunds, *The Shawnee Prophet* [Lincoln: University of Nebraska Press, 1985], 33).

"Zen Suicide." Poem by Richard from 1979.

> My mother raised me
> A Lutheran
> For her sake,
> Old now,
> I cannot swallow
> The muzzle.
> Let us sing!

Richard's mother called Joel her "foster son." See **Prell, Ruth Sosin** and **Mother's Day**.

The line joining itself becomes a circle. See **Alpha**.

AUTHOR'S NOTE

This work attempts to be accurate in its facts, with one exception: I have, for the sake of the essential story, combined two of Joel's residences.

ACKNOWLEDGMENTS

This book could not have been written without the profound support of Gale, Leigh, and Richard. I can't say enough, and so I say very little.

The Virginia Center for the Creative Arts generously offered me a residency when I was working on an early draft of the book.

Gratefully acknowledged are the journals in which versions of this material originally appeared: "The Dead Dog Essay," in the *Florida Review*; "Binoculars," in the *Southeast Review*; "Return Baggage," in *Rock & Sling*; "Death's Acres," in *Under the Sun*; "Spoon Altar," in *Tampa Review*; "The Bed of Metamorphosis," in *Fourth Genre*; "*Buteo regalis*" (as "Oh You and Your Deaths") in *Fraglit*; and the final breakthrough essay, "Companion to an Untold Story," in *The Pinch*.